From Farmland to Card Shop

A History of Shadyside Through the Windows of 5522 Walnut St.

By: Jason Kirin

Introduction

In May of 2022 I began a research project regarding the life of my biological grandmother, Shirley Cavanaugh. I purchased a membership to Newspapers.com and started collecting articles that mentioned her. As I sat scouring these archives a thought occurred to me... My wife's birthday was approaching. Could I find something in these archives that would serve well as a gift? After all, I knew the address, 5522 Walnut St., where her business, Kards Unlimited, is has some interesting history to it. Not the least of which was during the 1950s when an after-hours speakeasy called the Hollywood Social Club was located on the second floor and, at some point, the mob was involved with ownership. Certainly I could find something. Perhaps an article I could print and frame or photograph I could colorize and restore? Either way I knew grandma Shirley would have to wait. In the search bar of Newspapers.com I typed "5522 Walnut St."

Within seconds 169 archived newspapers loaded, chronologically, before me. Confused, I sat for a moment staring at the first result: The Pittsburgh Press, Wednesday April 12th, 1893. Surely that couldn't be correct. The first mention of 5522 Walnut St. in a newspaper was... 129 years ago?

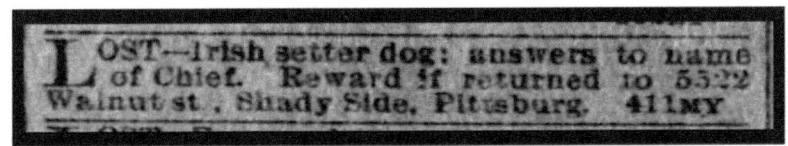

Soon it was apparent, 5522 Walnut St. was, at first, a home. A home, I would come to learn, with a front and rear address. Complete with a backyard. People lived and loved between its walls as early as the 1890s and as recent as the 1940s. No fewer than 9 businesses have operated out of this address from 1893 to the present day.

Reading through these articles wove a tapestry through my heart. A warp and weft of unbroken threads stretching as far back as 1868 began to unspool before me. There was magic here. There was love. There was death. But most importantly, there was, and is, a community spanning generations that stretches the entire reach of Walnut St. and beyond into Shadyside proper.

This book is that tapestry. Stitched together by newspaper clippings, uncovered photographs, ancestry research and narrative histories that have been woven by the threads of Shadyside's history.

A tapestry that is a gift to my wife, Amanda Blair.

10.11.22
Jason M. Kirin

5522 Walnut St.
Part 1: Early History

1868 - 1893

Our journey begins in 1868 when the city of Pittsburgh absorbed a farm owned by Rachel Aiken and her cousin-husband Thomas Aiken. Apparently it was the land's pleasantness that inspired the Shadyside name.

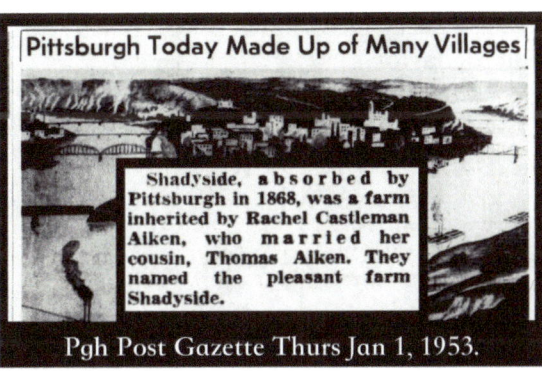

Pgh Post Gazette Thurs Jan 1, 1953.

Moving into 1872 as plots, lots and properties began to grow borders, a series of commonly known Pittsburgh names began to grace the pages of these historically archived maps.

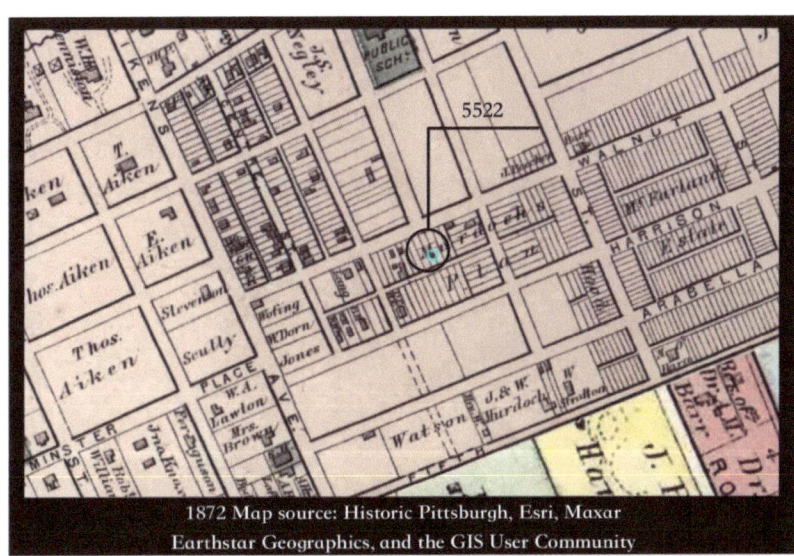

1872 Map source: Historic Pittsburgh, Esri, Maxar Earthstar Geographics, and the GIS User Community

Names such as Murdock; an early Pittsburgh family who, since 1840, had been homesteading in and around Squirrel Hill. This was another one of their properties.

1882 Map source: Historic Pittsburgh, Esri, Maxar
Earthstar Geographics, and the GIS User Community

Then, between 1882 and 1890, philanthropist William Thaw, a businessman who made his fortune in transportation, banking and property ownership, purchased lots 32 and 33 of Murdock's Plan.

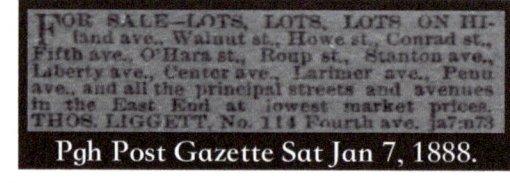

FOR SALE—LOTS, LOTS, LOTS ON Highland ave., Walnut st., Howe st., Conrad st., Fifth ave., O'Hara st., Roup st., Stanton ave., Liberty ave. Center ave. Larimer ave., Penn ave., and all the principal streets and avenues in the East End at lowest market prices. THOS. LIGGETT, No. 114 Fourth ave. ja7:n73

Pgh Post Gazette Sat Jan 7, 1888.

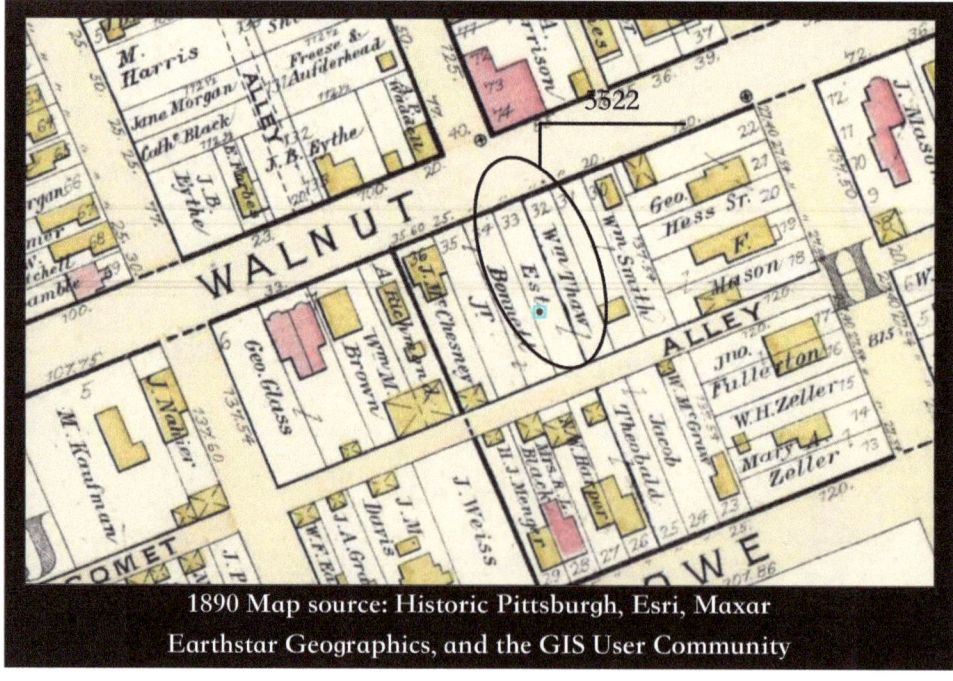

1890 Map source: Historic Pittsburgh, Esri, Maxar
Earthstar Geographics, and the GIS User Community

Interestingly - Thaw's grandson Lt. Colonel William Thaw II was one of, if not the first, American to engage in aerial combat in WW1 and with 5 confirmed aerial kills Thaw held the title of "Flying-Ace."

At some point he and his squadron pooled their funds together to purchase a lion as a mascot, they named him Whiskey.

Soon they bought a second one. They named him Soda.

Photo and story source: https://thelafayetteescadrille.org/whiskey-soda

By 1890 Emil Sitz became the owner of both lot 32 and 33. In December of 1890 Sitz was granted a permit to build a brick two story home with a mansard dwelling on the third floor. In 1892 Sitz sold this house to John J. Benzenhoefer. Now plot 33 was becoming a home. A home that was given the address...

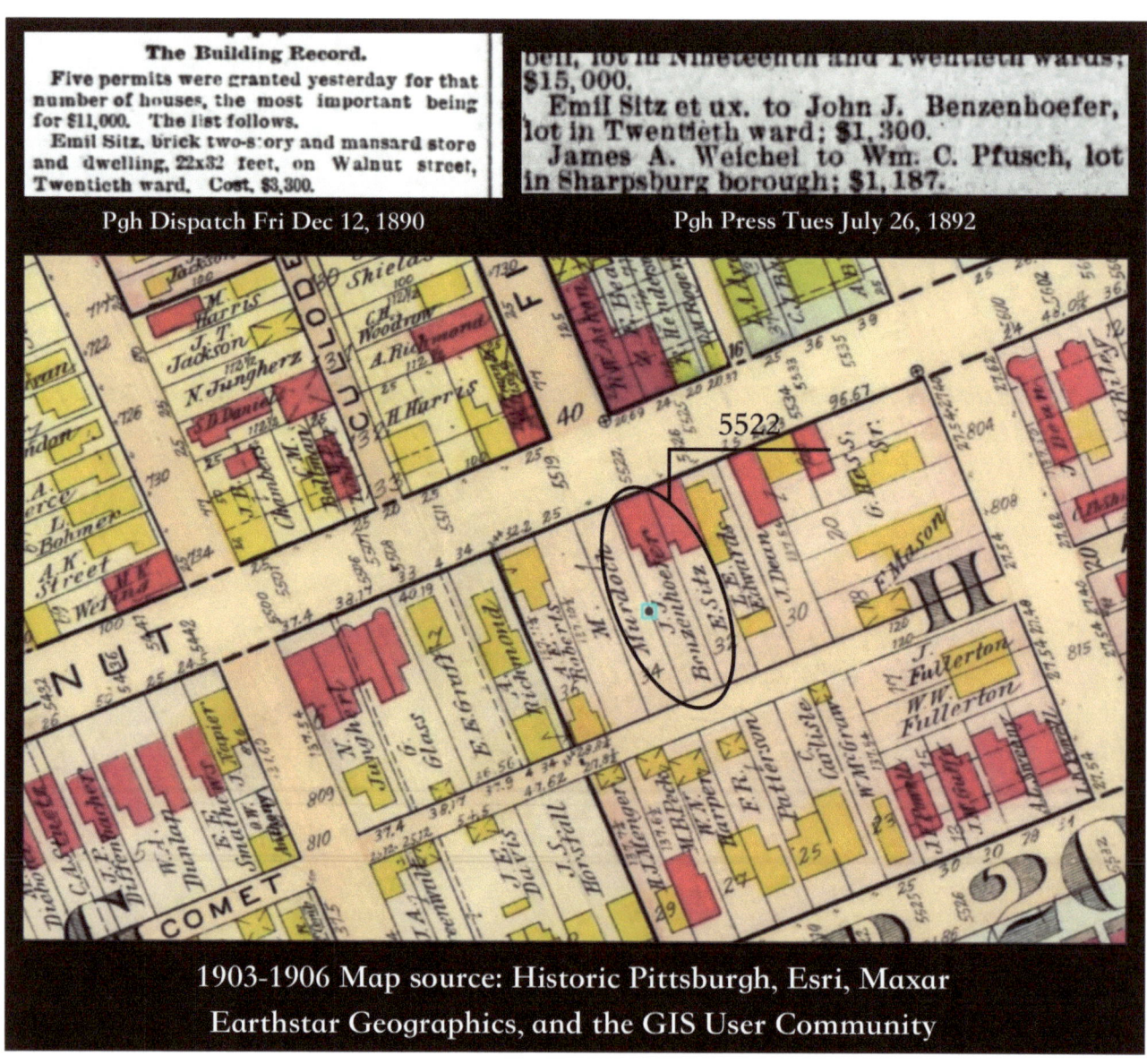

The Building Record.

Five permits were granted yesterday for that number of houses, the most important being for $11,000. The list follows.

Emil Sitz, brick two-story and mansard store and dwelling, 22x32 feet, on Walnut street, Twentieth ward. Cost, $3,300.

Pgh Dispatch Fri Dec 12, 1890

bell, lot in Nineteenth and Twentieth wards; $15,000.

Emil Sitz et ux. to John J. Benzenhoefer, lot in Twentieth ward; $1,300.

James A. Weichel to Wm. C. Pfusch, lot in Sharpsburg borough; $1,187.

Pgh Press Tues July 26, 1892

1903-1906 Map source: Historic Pittsburgh, Esri, Maxar Earthstar Geographics, and the GIS User Community

...5522 Walnut Street, Pittsburg Pa.

5522 Walnut St.
Part 2: (R)esidential History

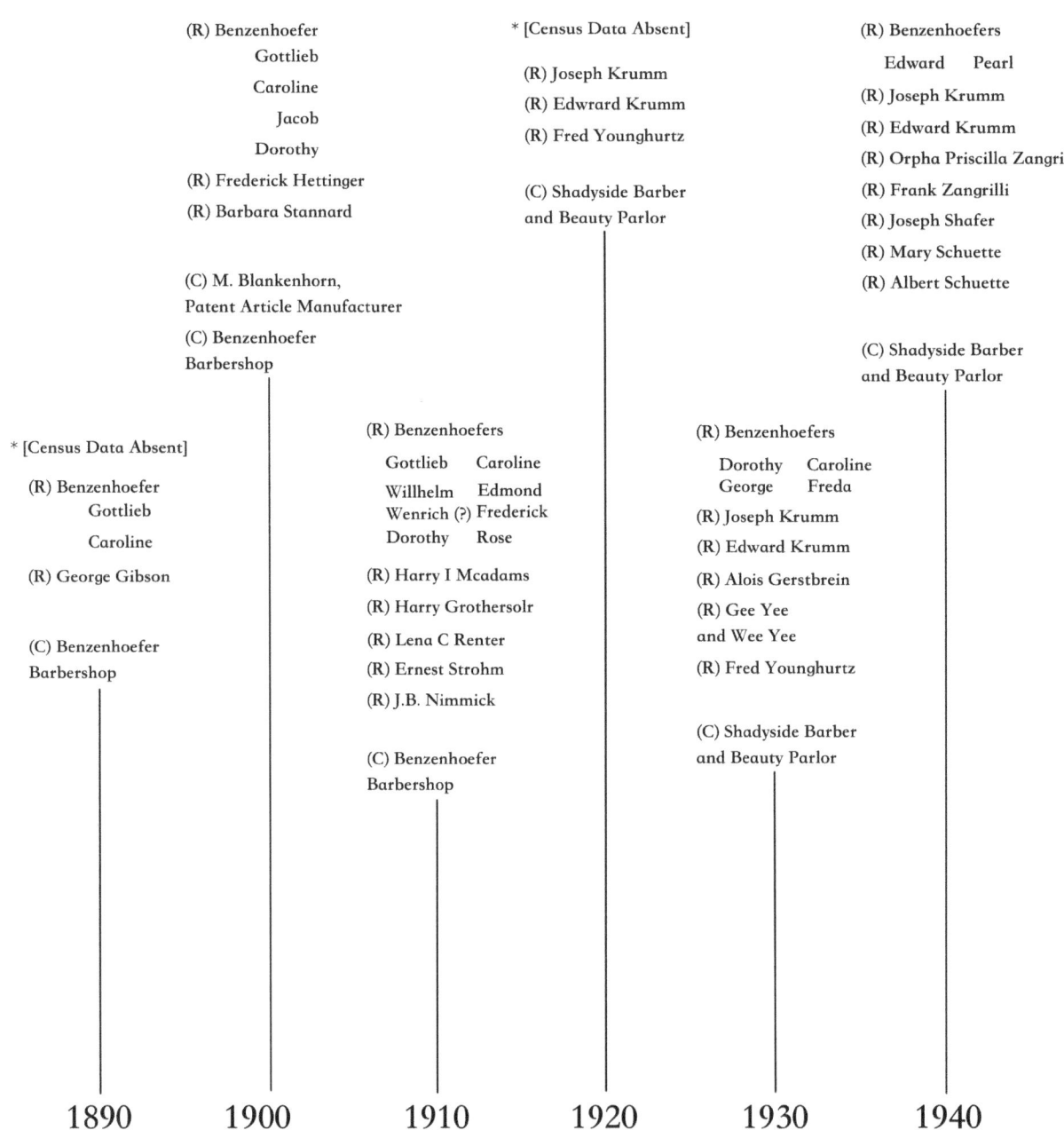

(R) Benzenhoefer
  Gottlieb
  Caroline
  Jacob
  Dorothy
(R) Frederick Hettinger
(R) Barbara Stannard

(C) M. Blankenhorn,
Patent Article Manufacturer
(C) Benzenhoefer
Barbershop

* [Census Data Absent]
(R) Benzenhoefer
  Gottlieb
  Caroline
(R) George Gibson

(C) Benzenhoefer
Barbershop

* [Census Data Absent]
(R) Joseph Krumm
(R) Edwrard Krumm
(R) Fred Younghurtz

(C) Shadyside Barber
and Beauty Parlor

(R) Benzenhoefers
  Gottlieb   Caroline
  Willhelm Edmond
  Wenrich (?) Frederick
  Dorothy   Rose
(R) Harry I Mcadams
(R) Harry Grothersolr
(R) Lena C Renter
(R) Ernest Strohm
(R) J.B. Nimmick

(C) Benzenhoefer
Barbershop

(R) Benzenhoefers
  Dorothy   Caroline
  George   Freda
(R) Joseph Krumm
(R) Edward Krumm
(R) Alois Gerstbrein
(R) Gee Yee
and Wee Yee
(R) Fred Younghurtz

(C) Shadyside Barber
and Beauty Parlor

(R) Benzenhoefers
  Edward   Pearl
(R) Joseph Krumm
(R) Edward Krumm
(R) Orpha Priscilla Zangrilli
(R) Frank Zangrilli
(R) Joseph Shafer
(R) Mary Schuette
(R) Albert Schuette

(C) Shadyside Barber
and Beauty Parlor

1890   **1900**   **1910**   **1920**   **1930**   **1940**

*1890 Census Data lost to fire in 1921
1920 Census taker <u>skipped</u> 5522 Walnut St.

1890 & 1920 information garnered from
newspaper archives, museum archives and
ancestry research.

Three things must be noted regarding the US Census information.

First, tragically, the 1890 US Population Census was almost entirely destroyed by fire and water damage in 1921.

Second, unfortunately, the 1920 Census data taker simply skipped 5522 Walnut Street. Altogether.

Third, luckily, 5522 Walnut St. was only residential from the 1890s until the 1940s and the census information for 1900, 1910, 1930 and 1940 are easily accessible.

When we intertwine available census data with ancestry research and newspaper archives, vignettes of the tenants' lives can be painted momentarily back into reality.

Allowing us a glimpse of moments that have passed in shared spaces that have transcended time.

George Gibson

As mentioned, the 1890 US Census was almost entirely lost to fire and water damage in 1921. Hence we learn of our first resident through experiences recorded in newspapers and other public documentation.

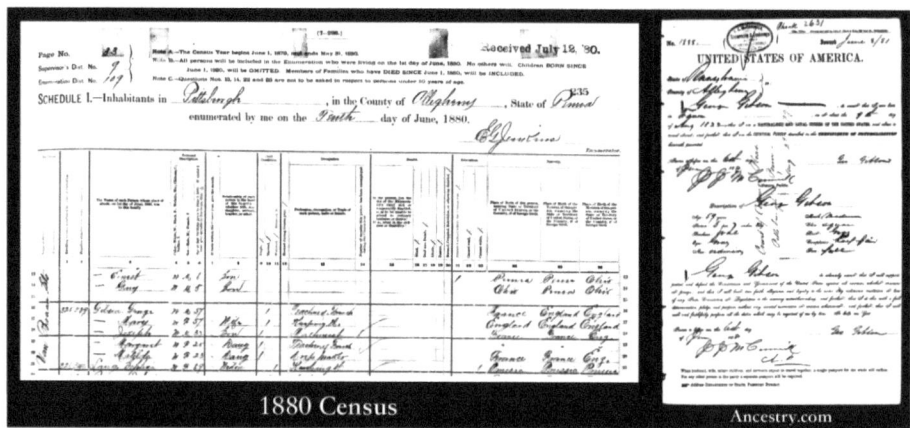

1880 Census

Ancestry.com

Having emigrated from France to Pittsburgh in 1881 Gibson would first take up residence at 325 Van Braam St. where, according to the 1880 census, he listed his occupation as Teacher of French.

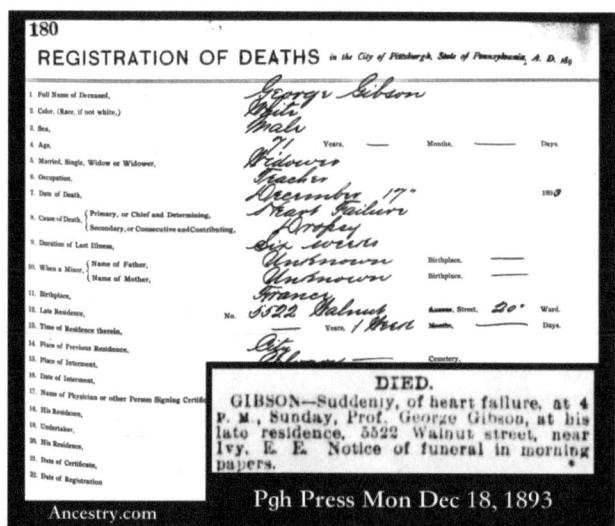

Pgh Press Mon Dec 18, 1893

Ancestry.com

We know of George Gibson as a resident due to his death notice listing his address as 5522 Walnut St.

Interestingly it isn't until the death notice of Gibson's daughter Marguerite in 1908 that we learn he was a professor at the Pennsylvania College for Women. A college that would change its name in 1957 to Chatham; possibly making his move from Van Braam St. to Walnut St. a matter of walking convenience.

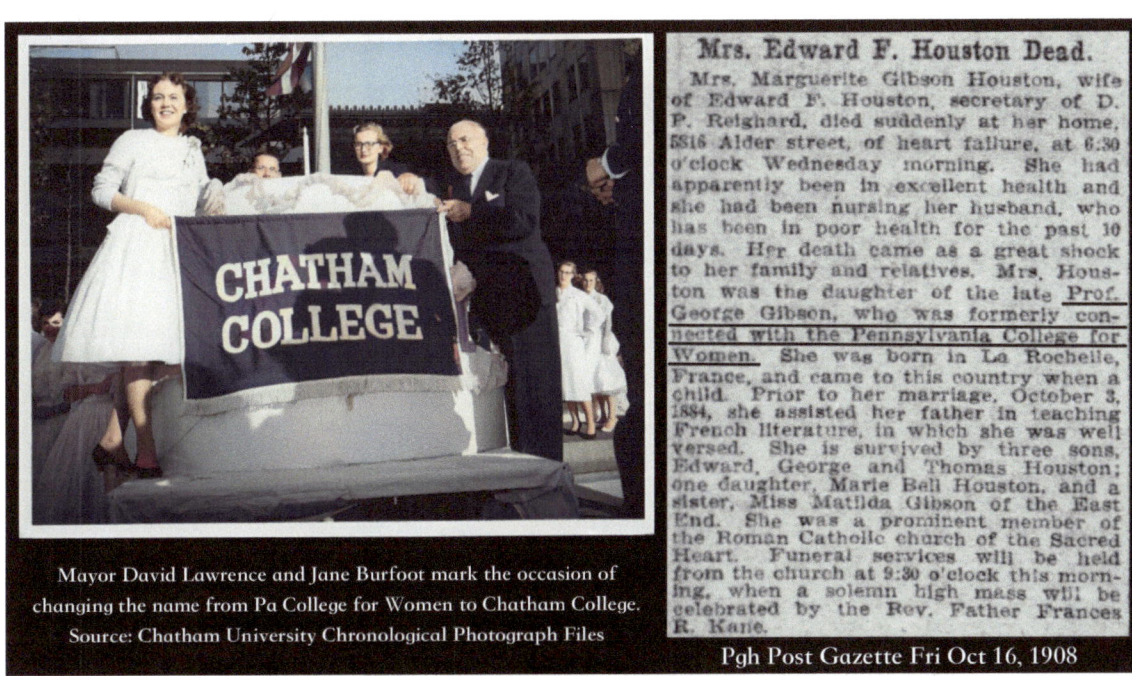

Mayor David Lawrence and Jane Burfoot mark the occasion of changing the name from Pa College for Women to Chatham College.
Source: Chatham University Chronological Photograph Files

Mrs. Edward F. Houston Dead.

Mrs. Marguerite Gibson Houston, wife of Edward F. Houston, secretary of D. P. Reighard, died suddenly at her home, 5816 Alder street, of heart failure, at 6:30 o'clock Wednesday morning. She had apparently been in excellent health and she had been nursing her husband, who has been in poor health for the past 10 days. Her death came as a great shock to her family and relatives. Mrs. Houston was the daughter of the late Prof. George Gibson, who was formerly connected with the Pennsylvania College for Women. She was born in La Rochelle, France, and came to this country when a child. Prior to her marriage, October 3, 1884, she assisted her father in teaching French literature, in which she was well versed. She is survived by three sons, Edward, George and Thomas Houston; one daughter, Marie Bell Houston, and a sister, Miss Matilda Gibson of the East End. She was a prominent member of the Roman Catholic church of the Sacred Heart. Funeral services will be held from the church at 9:30 o'clock this morning, when a solemn high mass will be celebrated by the Rev. Father Frances R. Kane.

Pgh Post Gazette Fri Oct 16, 1908

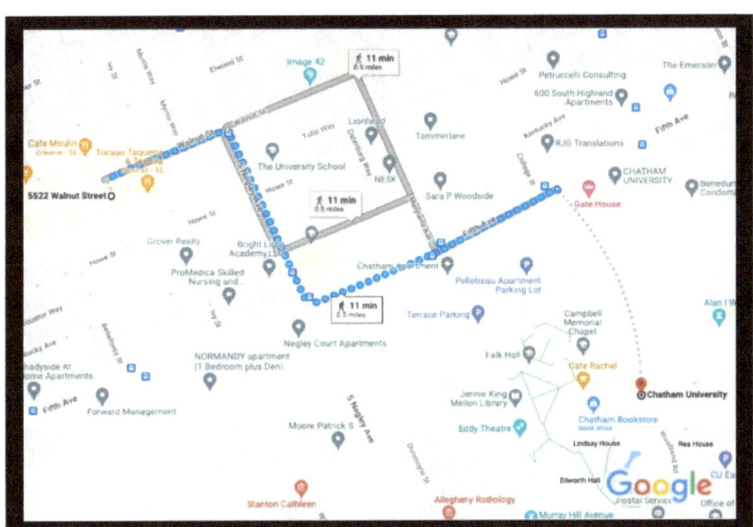

The Benzenhoefers

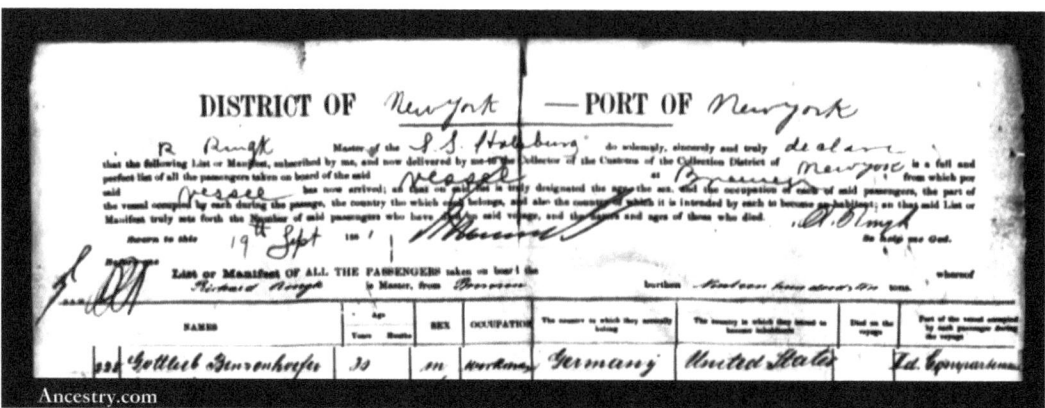

DISTRICT OF *New York* — PORT OF *New York*

In 1881 Gottlieb Benzenhoefer arrived in New York city on a boat set out from Germany.* Althought the next 10 years of Gottlieb's life are opaque he ultimately moved to Pittsburgh around by 1893.

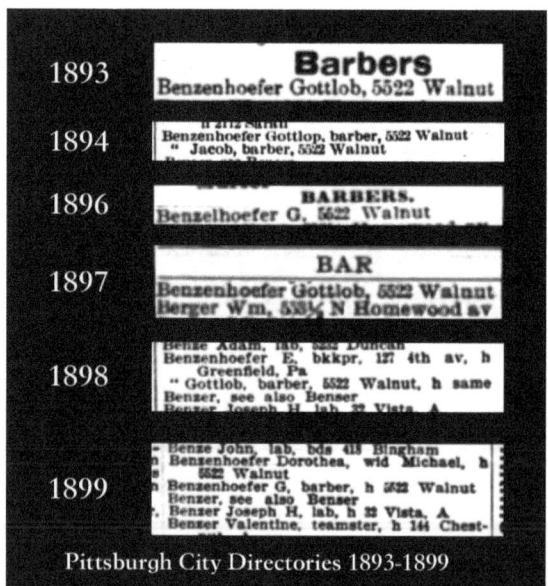

1893	**Barbers** Benzenhoefer Gottlob, 5522 Walnut
1894	Benzenhoefer Gottlop, barber, 5522 Walnut " Jacob, barber, 5522 Walnut
1896	**BARBERS.** Benzelhoefer G, 5522 Walnut
1897	**BAR** Benzenhoefer Gottlob, 5522 Walnut Berger Wm, 535½ N Homewood av
1898	Benzenhoefer E, bkkpr, 127 4th av, h Greenfield, Pa " Gottlob, barber, 5522 Walnut, h same Benzer, see also Benser
1899	Bensenhoefer Dorothea, wid Michael, h 5522 Walnut Benzenhoefer G, barber, h 5522 Walnut Benzer, see also Benser

Pittsburgh City Directories 1893-1899

Contending with the information lost when the 1890 census was destroyed in a 1921 fire, we turn our attention to the R.L. Polk & Company Pittsburgh City Directories. (Most of which are available to peruse at the Detre Library & Archives at the Heinz History Center.)

From these directories we can verify that during the 1890s not only did Gottlieb live at 5522 Walnut St. but he also ran his business as a barber out of the same address.

*According to an article on http://www.norwayheritage.com/ this journey would have taken Gottlieb approximately 9 days.

MARRIAGE LICENSE DOCKET.

Series C.
No. 8090

Gottlob Benzenhoefer born in Germany on the 17" day of Aug: A. D. 1866 residing at 5522 Walnut St, Pgh, Pa, occupation Barber, not related by blood or marriage to the person whom he desires to marry has not been married before

Caroline Hilkert born in Germany on the 16" day of Oct: A. D. 1873 residing at East St, Allegheny, Pa, occupation has not been married before

Marriage License issued Nov 2" 1896

Consent of _____, residing at _____
Consent of _____, residing at _____
Consent Filed _____ 189_; Married Nov 3" 1896
By Rev. Fried: Braud: Duplicate certificate returned Nov 10" 1896

Furthermore, an 1896 Marriage License Docket has both Gottlieb and his spouse Caroline Hilkert listed as living at the Benzenhoefer family home at 5522 Walnut St.

Caroline & Gottlieb Benzenhoefer
Source: Ancestry.com

From the 1900 Census we see that no fewer than 5 Benzenhoefer's live at 5522 Walnut St.

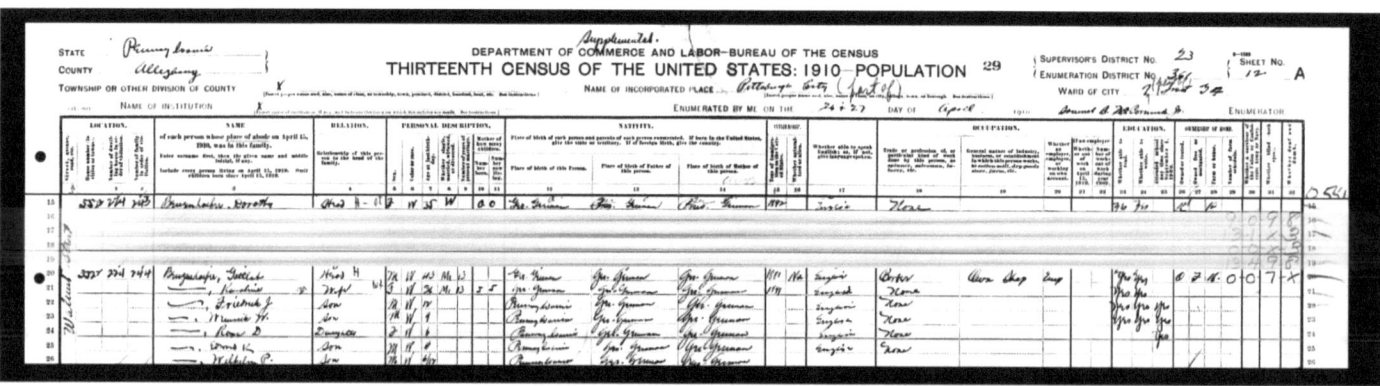

From the 1910 Census we see that number climb to 8.

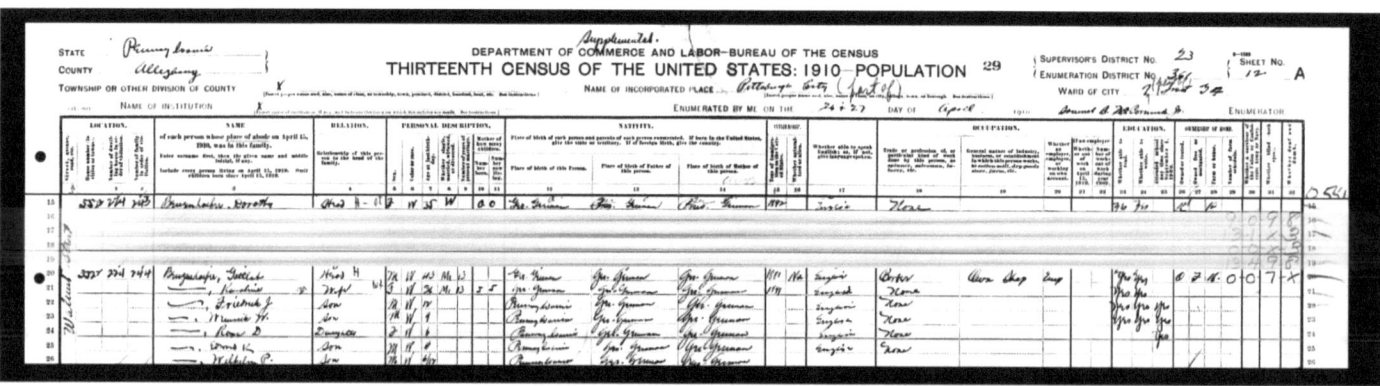

From the 1930 Census we see that number move down to 4.

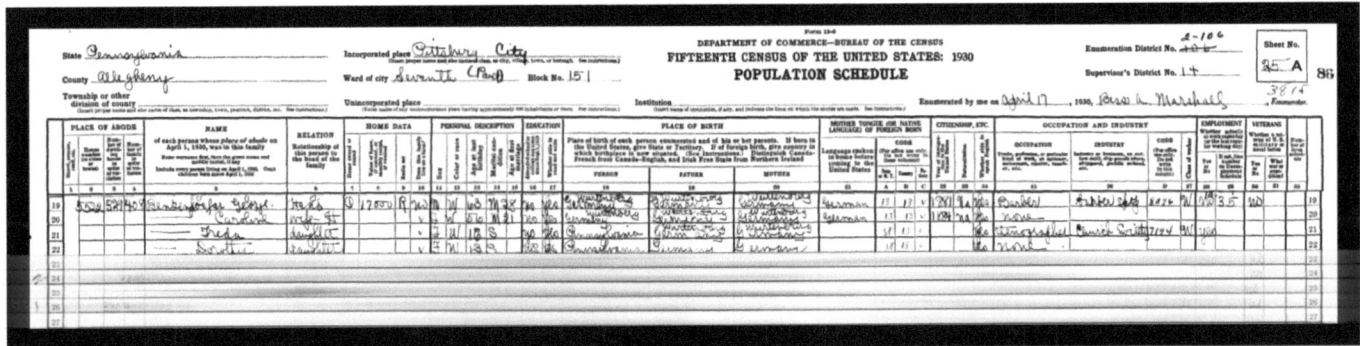

By the 1940s, as Walnut St. began to commercialize further, of the Benzenhoefers only Edward and Pearl remained.

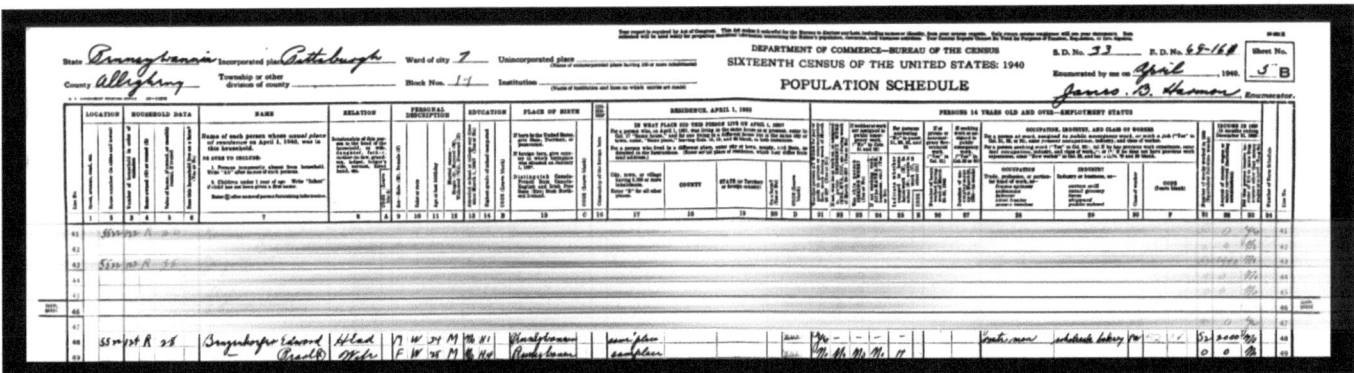

During those years...

A tragedy occurred on March 15, 1912:

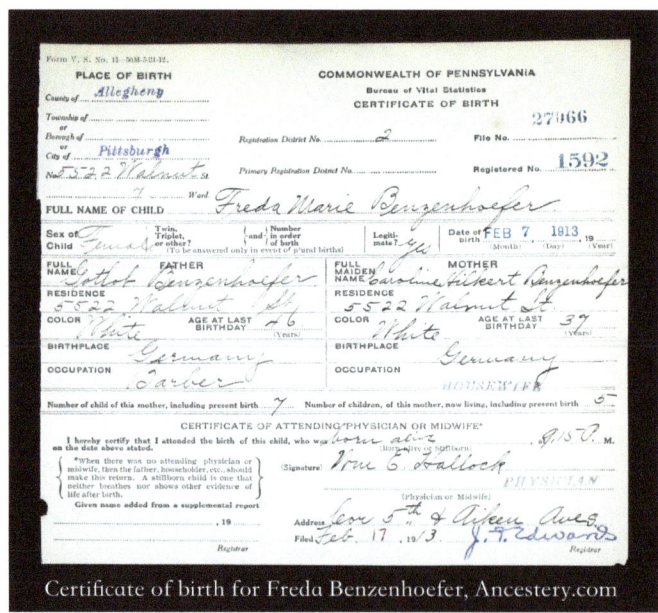

Certificate of birth for Infant Benzenhoefer, Ancestery.com

Certificate of death for Infant Benzenhoefer, Ancestery.com

In 1913, life:

Certificate of birth for Freda Benzenhoefer, Ancestery.com

In 1931, love.

Miss Freda Benzenhoefer Weds Mr. Guy M. Beaty In Pittsburgh

Young Couple to Make Trip Through North and in Florida Before Coming to Charlotte to Make Their Home.

A wedding of cordial interest to a wide circle of friends in this city was that of Miss Freda Benzenhoeffer of Pittsburgh, Pa., and Guy M. Beaty, Jr., of this city, which was solemnized last Saturday evening at the home of the bride's parents, Mr. and Mrs. G. Benzenhoeffer, at 5522 Walnut street, Pittsburgh, Pa.

The bride was given in marriage by her father and the bridegroom had as his best man Ed Benzenhoeffer, brother of the bride.

Rev. A G. Merkins, of the Lutheran church, pastor of the bride, officiated.

The bride was attired in light blue taffeta and carried a white Bible that was given her by her parents when she was confirmed. Her only ornament was a star pendant a gift of the bridegroom.

Relatives and a few intimate friends attended the wedding which was followed by a charming and informal reception.

The young couple left for a trip through the north and will later visit Florida after which they will be at home in Charlotte.

The bride was educated in the Pittsburgh school and is a bright and accomplished young woman. She was secretary to Dr. W. C. Chappell of the Pittsburgh Baptist association. She has been active in young peoples work in the Lutheran church and secretary of the Sunday school.

The bridegroom is the son of Mr. and Mrs. Guy M. Beaty of this city. He was educated in the city schools and specialized in mechanical engineering at Carnegie Tech at Pittsburgh. He is associated in business with his father contractor-distributor of pipe and boiler coverings in this city.

The Charlotte Observer Friday, July 3, 1931

Ultimately Gottlieb died in 1937 and Caroline, 364 days later, in 1938.

Death Certificate source: Ancestry.com

*The misspelling Gottlob is pervasive and ended up being the name on his gravestone.

I often think about Caroline and Gottlieb. The lives they must have lived under the same roof, between the same walls I find myself so often living. I stand near the poetry books, I draw my fingers along the shelf, I hear the floorboards creak beneath me. The same floorboards I know they too walked across. I'm not entirely certain how I feel about ghosts. I know little about spirits. I know, however, they are still here. A part of them remains. A part of them lives on in Kards Unlimited.

The Benzenhoefer Family at 5522 Walnut St. in 1908.
Contrasted against 5522 Walnut St. in 2022.
Photo source: Ancestry.com

According to the 1900 Census, Barbara Stannard was a 34 year old roomer. While living at 5522 Walnut St. she worked as a dressmaker.

Stannard also taught night classes in dressmaking and costuming at Carnegie Tech. Moreover, she taught sewing and cooking at the North Continuation School.

From 1916 to 1929, Miss Stannard taught sewing and cooking in the old North Continuation School, and she organized and taught sewing in evening classes at Carnegie Tech.

Pgh Press Wed Jan 15, 1947

ND SECTION—PAG

RNEGIE TECH ENJOYS OUTING

Girls Win Chicken Fight.

The Misses Mary Wight and Lorna Mc-Williams were victors in a chicken fight, receiving for their prowess a horn and sword, both tin of course, while the spoon and lemon race was won by Miss Jane Lillian Caldwell.

Among the faculty members were Director A. A. Hamerschlag, Dean John H. Leet, Dean C. B. Connelley, Dean C. R. Howlett, Secretary William P. Field, Dr. W. H. Libby, Prof. F. F. McIntosh, Herbert S. Sill, Prof. John T. Morris, Hugh A. Calderwood, Dr. E. H. Harris, W. H. Dosey, W. H. Megers, E. L. Burby, W. A. Wood, J. H. McCulloch, Arthur C. Burgoyne, Sr., J. H. Weidlein, Paul H. Dorweiler, Ralph Holmes, Vernon Sollom, Frank Orbin, A. W. Tarbell and the Misses Barbara Stannard, Marion Patton, Catherine Eastman, Bessie Merrill and Janet Van Hise.

Pgh Post Gazette Sun May 25, 1913

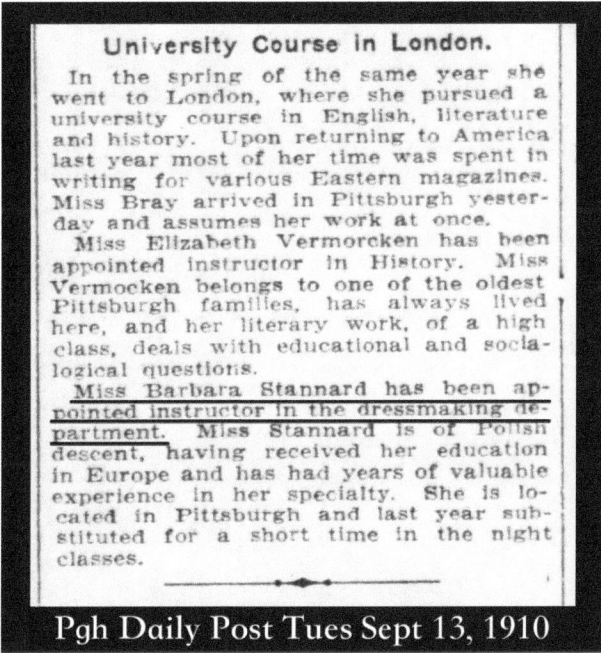

University Course in London.

In the spring of the same year she went to London, where she pursued a university course in English, literature and history. Upon returning to America last year most of her time was spent in writing for various Eastern magazines. Miss Bray arrived in Pittsburgh yesterday and assumes her work at once.

Miss Elizabeth Vermorcken has been appointed instructor in History. Miss Vermorcken belongs to one of the oldest Pittsburgh families, has always lived here, and her literary work, of a high class, deals with educational and socialogical questions.

Miss Barbara Stannard has been appointed instructor in the dressmaking department. Miss Stannard is of Polish descent, having received her education in Europe and has had years of valuable experience in her specialty. She is located in Pittsburgh and last year substituted for a short time in the night classes.

Pgh Daily Post Tues Sept 13, 1910

1899	Stannard Barbara, h 5522 Walnut
1902	Dress Makers Stannard Barbara 5522 Walnut
1903	Dressmakers. Stannard Barbara 5522 Walnut
1909	DRESSMAKERS Stannard Barbara R 5135 5th av

Pittsburgh City Directories 1899-1909

She lived and worked at 5522 Walnut St. as a personalized dressmaker and by the 1900s Barbara had opened her own dress shop on 5th Ave.

Here's 'Bee Line' Five Miles Long

A retired teacher of Pittsburg has 525.000 pets.

They are the bees she has tended for 15 years. If someone were patient enough and sufficiently cautious to place them they would make a line about five miles long.

A depression, it seems, has hit the bees and they grumble about it, according to Miss Barbara R. Stannard of 700 Graphic Street. The long spells of rain this spring kept the bees indoors, preventing them from collecting honey from fruit blossoms.

"When I was a little girl in Germany," Miss Stannard said, "I was given a book of bee stories. I have been studying them ever since, more than 60 years.

"I don't try to make any money from my bees. I love them and just keep them for pets."

Pgh Press Sun July 26, 1931

KEEPER OF THE BEES

MISS BARBARA R. STANNRAD—Fearlessly handling a swarm of bees outside her home in Greenfield. Miss Stannard is 72, one of the hundreds of beekeepers in Allegheny County.

Pgh Sun Telegraph Mon Nov 8, 1937

OLDEST KEEPER HERE

"Clustering" at the moment are the bees of Miss Barbara R. Stannard, Pittsburgh's oldest woman beekeeper. At her home at 700 Graphic Street, Greenfield, 71-year-old Miss Stannard has 10 colonies. Honey produced by her bees won a prize at the recent Allegheny County Fair. Active for her age, Miss Stannard still tends her bees and extracts the honey herself. However, she is seeking a buyer for her apiary because she is no longer able to care for the bees as she wishes. Her new interest is canary birds which she raises and sells.

Miss Stannard's interest in bees dates back to a child's illustrated bee book. But it wasn't until she installed her own beeyard in 1912 that she got a closeup of a bee. She explains why she took up beekeeping:

"Beekeeping is one way to 'Live Alone and Like It.' Having something to do is a way to forget your troubles. Too, bees provide an interesting study and bee behavior is something unusual. I would like to keep them but while the spirit is willing the body is wearing out."

Several brothers and sisters reside in the United States and she sees them "once in a while," but she says she will continue to live alone, baking her own bread, reading, writing and tending to her bees and canaries.

ALSO AN ARTIST

Too, she is doing a little drawing and painting. Last winter, she took a few drawing lessons and is offering encouragement to several youngsters who would ʹ e to become artists.

Pgh Sun Telegraph
Mon Nov 8, 1937

In her spare time as a teacher at Carnegie Tech, Barbara Stannard studied architecture. By the 1920s she designed, and had built, the first corrugated iron house in Pittsburgh. There she retired to not only take up painting and canary raising but also follow her childhood love for bees; creating a small apiary sanctuary for a colony of, sometimes depressed and grumbling, 525,000 bees.

She came to Pittsburgh in 1897, organized and taught sewing in evening classes at Carnegie Tech and in between times studied architecture. The latter led to the erection of the first corrugated iron home in the city. It was prefabricated in St. Paul along lines designated by the little old lady who a neighbor described as: "Kind and considerate to all."

Harrisburg Telegraph Thurs, Jan16, 1947

Barbara Stannard died January 11, 1947. In her will she decreed her entire estate (2 dwellings and a lot equalling $12,000) be left to "assist fatherless girls in securing vocational or other educational training to help them support themselves." She also left her 7 canaries (only 3 of them good singers mind you) to the neighborhood insurance collector. Her apiary was to be moved to the Saint Barnabas Home.

EX-TEACHER WILLS $12,000 TO GIRLS

The little old lady who lived in the little tin house in Greenfield today had left a $12,000 estate for the education and support of fatherless girls.

Miss Barbara R. Stannard, 80, a pensioned school teacher, specified the fund should be administered by the judge of Juvenile Court and the superintendent of public schools.

She bequeathed all her household goods to her neighbors. Her seven canaries—three of them "good singers"—went to the neighborhood insurance collector, John F. Reilly.

GAVE AWAY APIARY

Some years ago she gave the apiary she had maintained at her home, 700 Graphic St., to St. Barnabas Home.

In her will filed today, Miss Stannard wrote she wanted her estate—two dwellings and three lots—put in trust to "assist fatherless girls in securing vocational or other educational training, designed to help them support themselves."

The Juvenile Court judge and the school superintendent are to have absolute discretion in choosing girls and the length of time they should be supported. Payments may be made directly to the girls, or to an educational institution or both.

The Peoples First National Bank and Trust Co. was named trustee for the fund.

FELT SORRY FOR GIRLS

Mrs. William J. Barron, 704 Graphic St., a neighbor for 25 years, said Miss Stannard, an artist, teacher and shop-keeper, had often told her:

"I feel sorry for homeless girls."

Mrs. Barron found Miss Stannard unconscious a week ago today. She died 12 hours later. She came to New York in 1887—ten years later to Pittsburgh. She had toured Europe with a sister of an Italian cardinal.

COSTUME DESIGNER

In New York she joined a stage group, designing and making costumes. From 1912 to 1939 she kept 10 colonies of bees. She taught sewing and cooking in old North Continuation School, Eighth St. and Duquesne Way, from 1916 to 1929. That school is now a vacant lot.

She operated a dress shop in the 5400 block Fifth Ave. in 1900 and sewed for some of Pittsburgh's richest families. She had 20 employes. Some continued to support in later life.

She chose the site of her house on a bluff overlooking Beechwood Blvd., designed the home and had it prefabricated in St. Paul. It was one of the first corrugated homes in the city. A brother, John M. Rehnee, St. Petersburg, Fla., said she had made several trips to Paris for trousseaus.

Pgh Sun Telegraph
Wed Jan 15, 1947

Teacher Leaves $12,000 To Aid Fatherless Girls

Estate of Kindly Woman, 80, to Be Used To Train Orphans to Support Themselves

Teaching and giving. Kindly Miss Barbara R. Stannard had done just that during most of her 80 years and she hasn't ended with death.

The little lady, who had an amazing curiosity for life even during her last years, left a $12,000 estate to be used for the education of fatherless girls, her will revealed yesterday.

She left the administering of her wishes up to the judge of juvenile court and the superintendent of schools. She said the fund was to be used:

"To assist fatherless girls in securing vocational or other educational training, designed to help them support themselves."

The money is to be given directly to the needy girls or to the institutions which they attend, or both. Miss Stannard, who lived in a corrugated iron home of her own design at 700 Graphic street, Greenfield, had lived a full and varied life. She came to Pittsburgh in 1897, organized and taught sewing in evening classes at Carnegie Tech and in between times studied architecture.

She operated a dress shop in the 5400 block of Fifth avenue and from 1916 to 1929, taught sewing and cooking at the old North Continuation school, Eighth street and Duquesne way.

Miss Stannard, who died a week ago, was a good neighbor and she bore that out in her will.

She bequeathed all her household goods to her neighbors and last but not least, she left her seven canaries—three of them "good singers," she pointed out—to the neighborhood insurance collector.

Pgh Post Gazette Thurs Jan 16, 1947

Fatherless Girls Benefit By Bequest

PITTSBURG, Jan. 15— (P) — The little old lady who lived in the little iron house high on the bluff overlooking Schenley Park left a $12,000 estate for the education and support of fatherless girls.

Miss Barbara R. Stannard, 80, who died a week ago, wrote in her will, filed today, that she wanted her estate — two dwellings and three lots put in trust to "assist fatherless girls in securing vocational or other educational training."

Altoona Trib Jan 16, 1947

J.B. Nimmick.

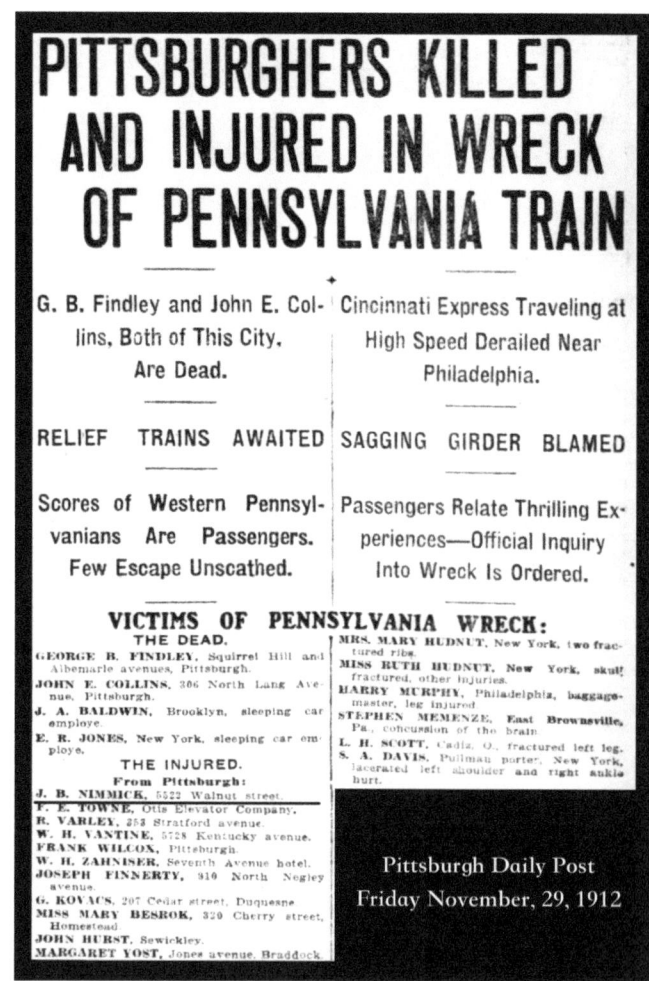

A Pittsburgher injured in the 1912 Glenloch Pennsylvania trainwreck. Nimmick is interesting and also complicated; the only accounts of the name J.B. Nimmick I can find are in relation to this trainwreck in 1912. In only one article their address is mentioned as 5522 Walnut St. No census information. Nothing to cross reference.

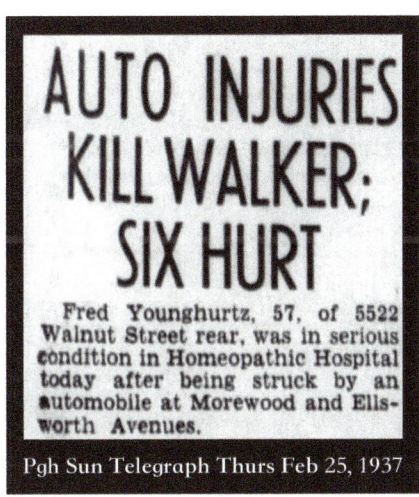

Pgh Sun Telegraph Thurs Feb 25, 1937

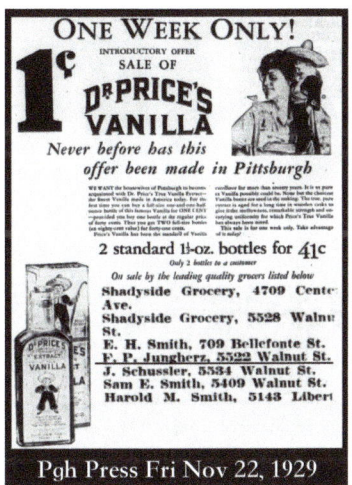

Pgh Press Fri Nov 22, 1929

While neither spelling Younghurtz nor Jungherz appears on any census records, there are 2 references to a Fred Youngurtz taking up residence at 5522 Walnut St. One is an account of him being a grocer and the other of a car accident he was injured in.

Photos Source: Shadyside Hospital Records, 1852-2008, MSS 1203, Detre Library and Archives, Heinz History Center

Youngurtz was taken to the Homeopathic Hospital in 1937 which would change its name one year later to the Shadyside Hospital and then 59 years later, become UPMC Shadyside.

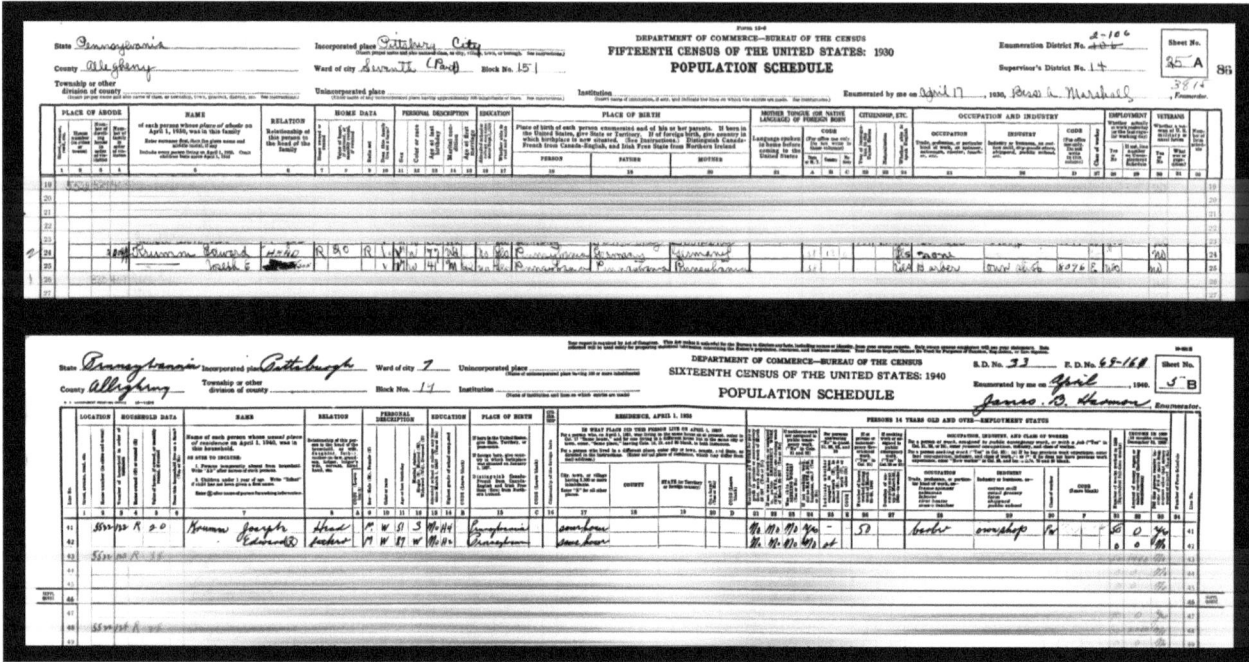

The Krumms have been especially interesting because the more information that is available, the more I am left with questions and less with answers.

Available census data, starting in 1860, allows us to follow Edward Krumm from the age of 8 until his eventual death at the age of 88.

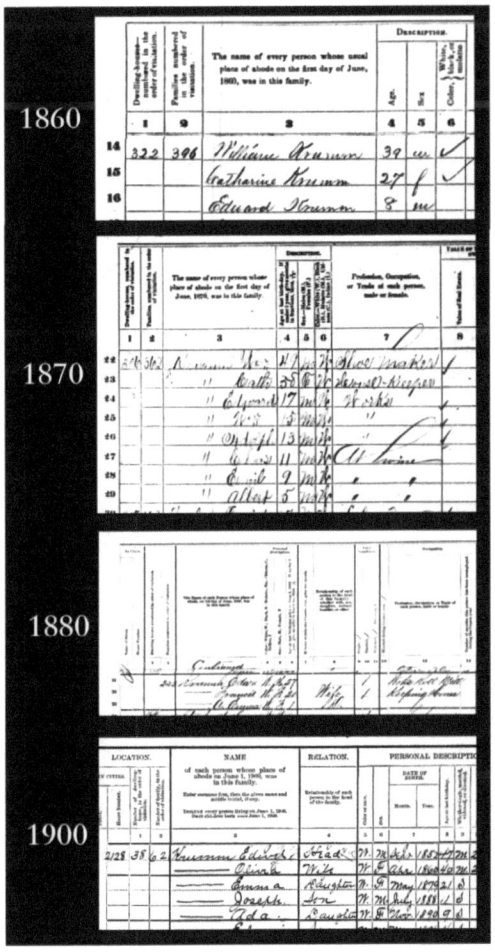

His father was a shoemaker named William. By the age of 17 Edward is listed on the 1870 census as a "worker." By 1880 Edward was married. His wife Francis Olivia Krumm died in 1913.

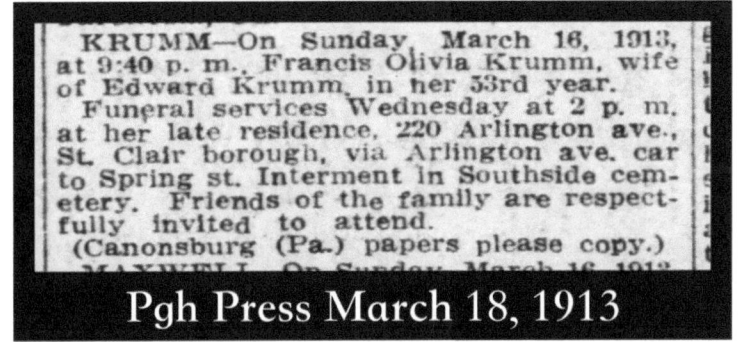

KRUMM—On Sunday, March 16, 1913, at 9:40 p. m., Francis Olivia Krumm, wife of Edward Krumm, in her 53rd year.

Funeral services Wednesday at 2 p. m. at her late residence, 220 Arlington ave., St. Clair borough, via Arlington ave. car to Spring st. Interment in Southside cemetery. Friends of the family are respectfully invited to attend.

(Canonsburg (Pa.) papers please copy.)

Pgh Press March 18, 1913

Together they had a son named Joseph. By 1900 47 year old Edward's occupation is listed as "iron worker" and Joseph was in school. I was unable to uncover a 1910 Census record for Krumm and, as mentioned earlier, the 1920s Census taker skipped 5522 Walnut Street. With what information we have in newspaper archives we can piece together the following.

Joseph started to take an interest in canoeing and camping. He takes out a few ads in search of an affordable canoe and soon thereafter begins to place multiple items for sale in the same paper...

A savage 22 caliber rifle, barber chair, large gas lamp, stencil outfit, 2 inch letters, ice skates and lady's high top outing shoes.

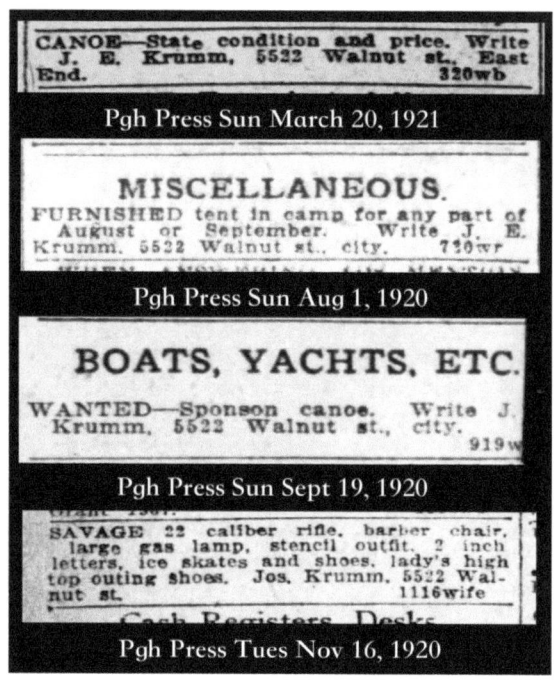

CANOE—State condition and price. Write J. E. Krumm, 5522 Walnut st., East End. 320wb

Pgh Press Sun March 20, 1921

MISCELLANEOUS.
FURNISHED tent in camp for any part of August or September. Write J. E. Krumm, 5522 Walnut st., city. 730wr

Pgh Press Sun Aug 1, 1920

BOATS, YACHTS, ETC.
WANTED—Sponson canoe. Write J. Krumm, 5522 Walnut st., city. 919w

Pgh Press Sun Sept 19, 1920

SAVAGE 22 caliber rifle, barber chair, large gas lamp, stencil outfit, 2 inch letters, ice skates and shoes, lady's high top outing shoes. Jos. Krumm, 5522 Walnut st. 1116wife

Pgh Press Tues Nov 16, 1920

The 1930 census reveals Edward Krumm, age 77, is still the head of house and Joseph is still a barber. The 1940 Census tells us that, indicated by the ⊗ next to Edward Krumm's name, he was the person who gave the information that day. Joseph is now the head of the house. At 87 Edward was not long for this world.

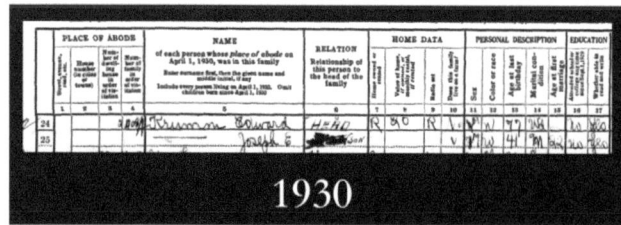

1930

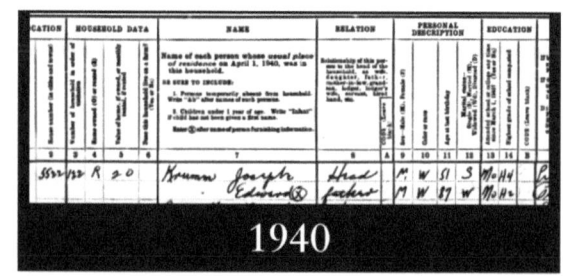

1940

On March 30, 1941 Edward Krumm died from a concussion he suffered 20 days earlier. According to the Pittsburgh Press, Krumm "stepped from the kitchen of his home into the rear yard March 10 and fell down <u>one</u> step, suffering the injury which caused his death."

Fall Leads to Death

A fall down one step proved fatal to Edward Krumm, 88, of <u>5522 Walnut St., East End,</u> who died in his home last night of a brain concussion. According to a report to the coroner, <u>Mr. Krumm stepped from the kitchen of his home into the rear yard</u> March 10 and fell down one step, suffering the injury which caused his death.

Pgh Press Mon March 31, 1941

Penn Pilot Program's 1939 Aerial Photographs

When I look at the Penn Pilot Program's 1939 Aerial Photographs of Shadyside it's interesting to see the single structure standing at the front of Walnut St. with the long empty corridor heading back towards Ivy. I consider where, inside of Kards Unlimited this "yard" must be. I assume it is near calendars, puzzles and journals.

Perhaps Krumm and the Benzenhoefers are the friendly ghosts who wander about adding charm and creekiness to the atmosphere of the store.

Joseph Shafer, Frank Zangrilli, Orpha Priscilla Zangrilli

Both Joseph and Frank's WWII draft cards showed up in a search and have interestingly conflicting information.

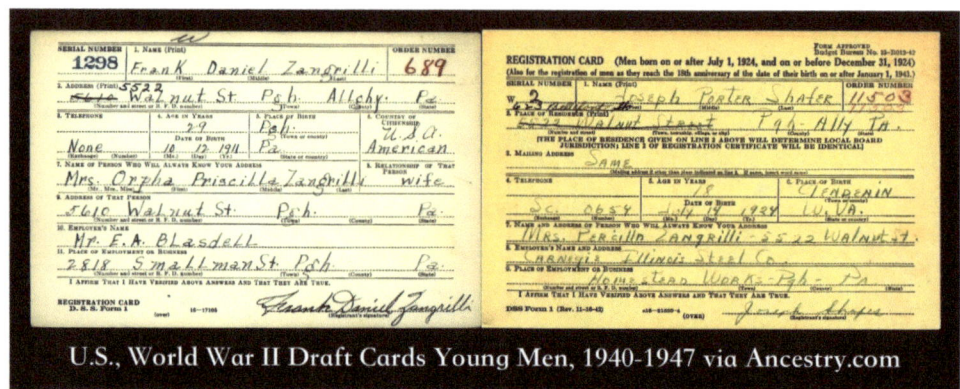

U.S., World War II Draft Cards Young Men, 1940-1947 via Ancestry.com

Frank lives at 5522 Walnut St. and the one person he trusts to always know his address is his wife Mrs. Orpha Priscilla Zangrilli who lives at 5610 Walnut St.

Joseph lives at ~~5522 Walnut St.~~ 623 Bellefonte St. and the one person he trusts to always know his address? Mrs. Percilla Zangrilli who lives at 5522 Walnut St.

Where, according to the 1940 census, they all lived at the same time.

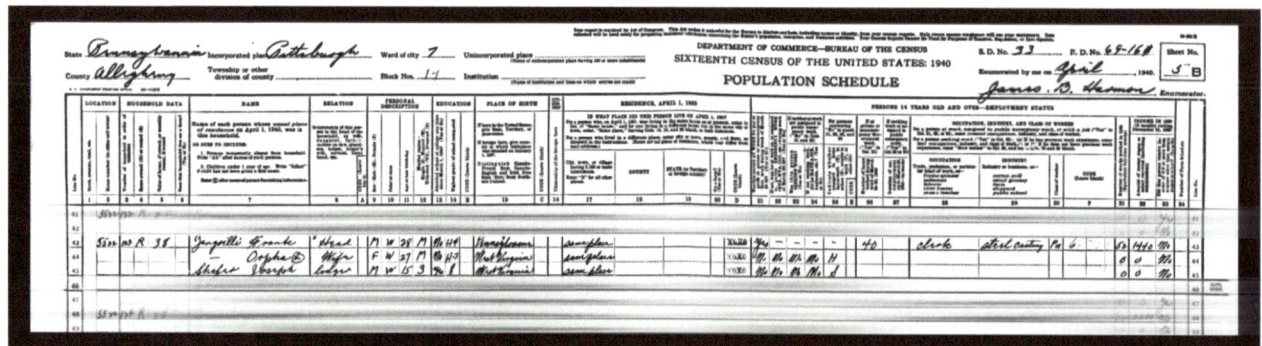

Honorable Mentions

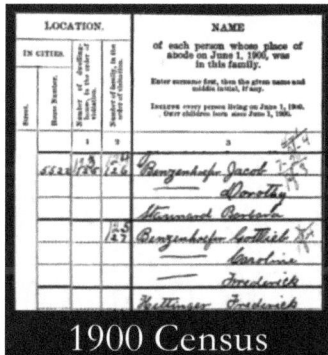
1900 Census

Fred H Hettinger Lodger, 16 yrs old, barber, emigrated from Germany in 1891. Nothing else turned up on this person

1910 Census

Lena C Renter Lodger, 22 yrs old, dressmaker (Barbara connection?) emigrated from Germany in 1902. Various name spellings still turn up nothing.

Ernst Strohm Lodger, 29 yrs old, machinist, chauffeur, emigrated from England in 1902. Nothing else turned up on this person

Harry Grothersolr Lodger, 29 yrs old, Chauffeur with Presste Auto, emigrated from England in 1902. Nothing else turned up on this person. Various name spellings still turn up nothing.

Harry Mcadams (middle initial is I or J, possibly t?) Lodger, Pittsburgh native, plumber. Nothing else turned up on this person

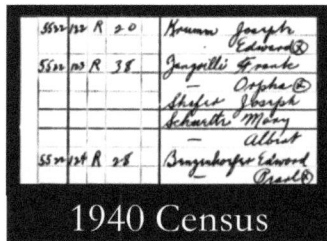
1930 Census

Alois Gerstbrein Lodger, 55 yrs old, butcher, emigrated from Germany in 1891. Nothing else turned up on this person
Gee Yee, (39) and **Wee Yee** (30) Brothers, California natives, owners and operators of a laundry shop. Nothing else turned up on either name.

1940 Census

Mary Schuette, 21 years old and husband **Albert Schuette**, 34 year old, painter.

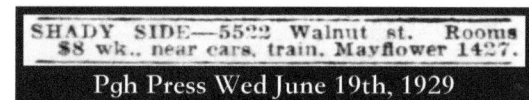
SHADY SIDE—5522 Walnut st. Rooms $8 wk., near cars, train. Mayflower 1427.
Pgh Press Wed June 19th, 1929

A nod of acknowledgement to all of the 1920s 8$/week lodgers though.

5522 Walnut St.
Part 3: (C)ommercial History

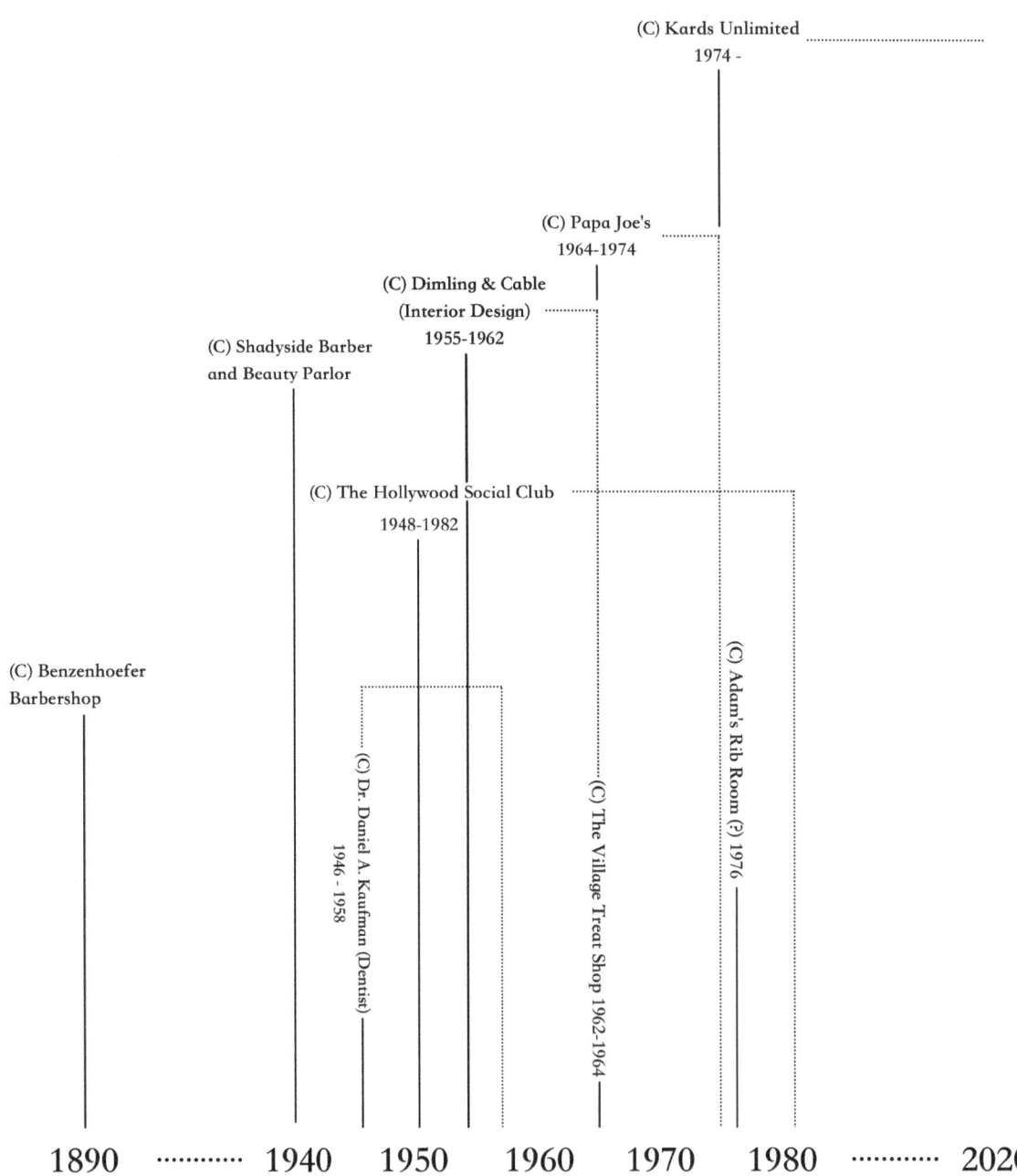

(C) Kards Unlimited
1974 -

(C) Papa Joe's
1964-1974

(C) Dimling & Cable
(Interior Design)
1955-1962

(C) Shadyside Barber
and Beauty Parlor

(C) The Hollywood Social Club
1948-1982

(C) Benzenhoefer
Barbershop

(C) Dr. Daniel A. Kaufman (Dentist)
1946 - 1958

(C) The Village Treat Shop 1962-1964

(C) Adam's Rib Room (?) 1976

1890 ·········· 1940   1950   1960   1970   1980 ·········· 2020

A note regarding photographs...

Throughout this book are a series of photos. Some of these photos have been archived and unseen since they were developed 40-50 years ago. Some of them were negatives or slides that I digitized. Often these photos were damaged, many of them were in black and white or grainy sepia tones.

While this project is, primarily, one of historical preservation it is also an attempt at historical restoration. As such each one of these photos has been repaired, enhanced and colorized digitally by me over the course of writing this book. Many of these photos are being shown here for the first time. None of this would have been possible without them.

At the end of this book you will find an extensive acknowledgement of each archive, each archivist and each photographer who helped in the creation of this journey.

A journey that begins February 19th, 1935 at the corner of Aiken Ave. and Walnut St.

Walnut St. and Aiken Ave.   Feb 19, 1935

SODA GRILL   Coca-Cola   CANDY-CIGARS

SCHILLER DRUG

Photo source: Pgh City Photographer Collection 1901-2000.

While 5522 remained a home until the late 1940s, by 1935 Walnut St. had become less residential and more commercial. From this eastward facing view of Walnut St. 5522 is a few blocks forward on the right. Among other places in this photo you can see the original Schiller's Drug sign.

Barbershop, Beauty Parlor. Patent Article Manufacturer.

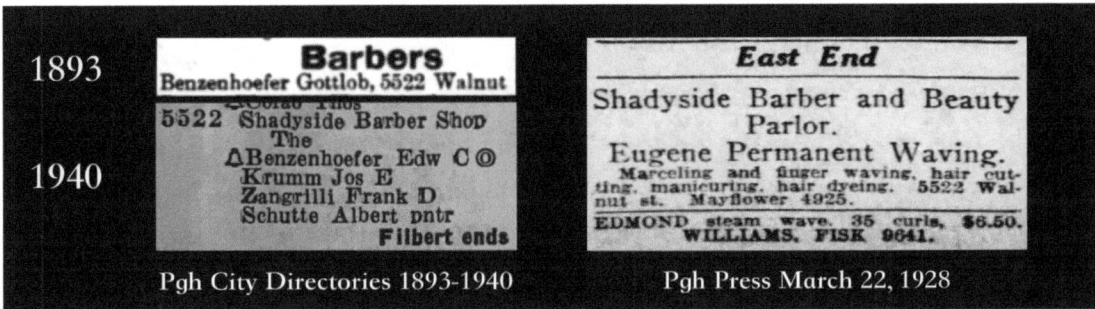

It's possible to find references as early as 1893 and as recent as 1940 to 5522 Walnut St as a barbershop or beauty parlor in some way.

In August of 1930 M. Blankenhorn placed 4 identical advertisements in the Pittsburgh Press to announce their services as a Patent Articles Manufacturer.

Dimling & Cable Inc.
Interior Designers

1955 - 1962

INTERIOR DESIGNERS
DIMLING & CABLE Inc.
5522 WALNUT STREET
PITTSBURGH 32, PENNSYLVANIA
MUseum 2-5550
Member of the American Institute of Decorators

DIMLING & CABLE INC.
5522 WALNUT STREET
PITTSBURGH 32 PENNSYLVANIA
MUseum 2-5550
Member of the
American Institute
of Decorators

DIMLING & CABLE, Inc.
—INTERIOR DESIGNERS—
5522 WALNUT STREET
MUseum 2-5550
Member of the
American Institute
of Decorators

Pgh Post Gazette ads from 1950s

The amount of lore, inspiration and love that surrounds Dimling & Cable could indeed fill an entire second book.

In the Post Gazette's December 12, 1981 article, "In Search of Good Taste," Dimling mentions being an avid collector of objects shaped like monkeys. He goes on to say that he has no design philosophy at all but rather, "guter geschmuck," which means "good taste" in German. Often he and his partner Charles Cable were known to perform puppet shows for their clients' children who came to visit their shop at 5522 Walnut St. In that same article one of his students is quoted as saying, "if Dimling's shop hadn't been there in the 1950s, Walnut wouldn't be what it is today."

It seems apparent that this was true for others as well...

While researching Dimling & Cable Inc. I found myself directed to the website 1stDibs.com. This website, among other things, is a place where sellers can auction away art. As I sat staring at this painting on my computer screen I felt a strange sense of uncanny valley. I knew I was looking at something familiar but it wasn't familiar at all.

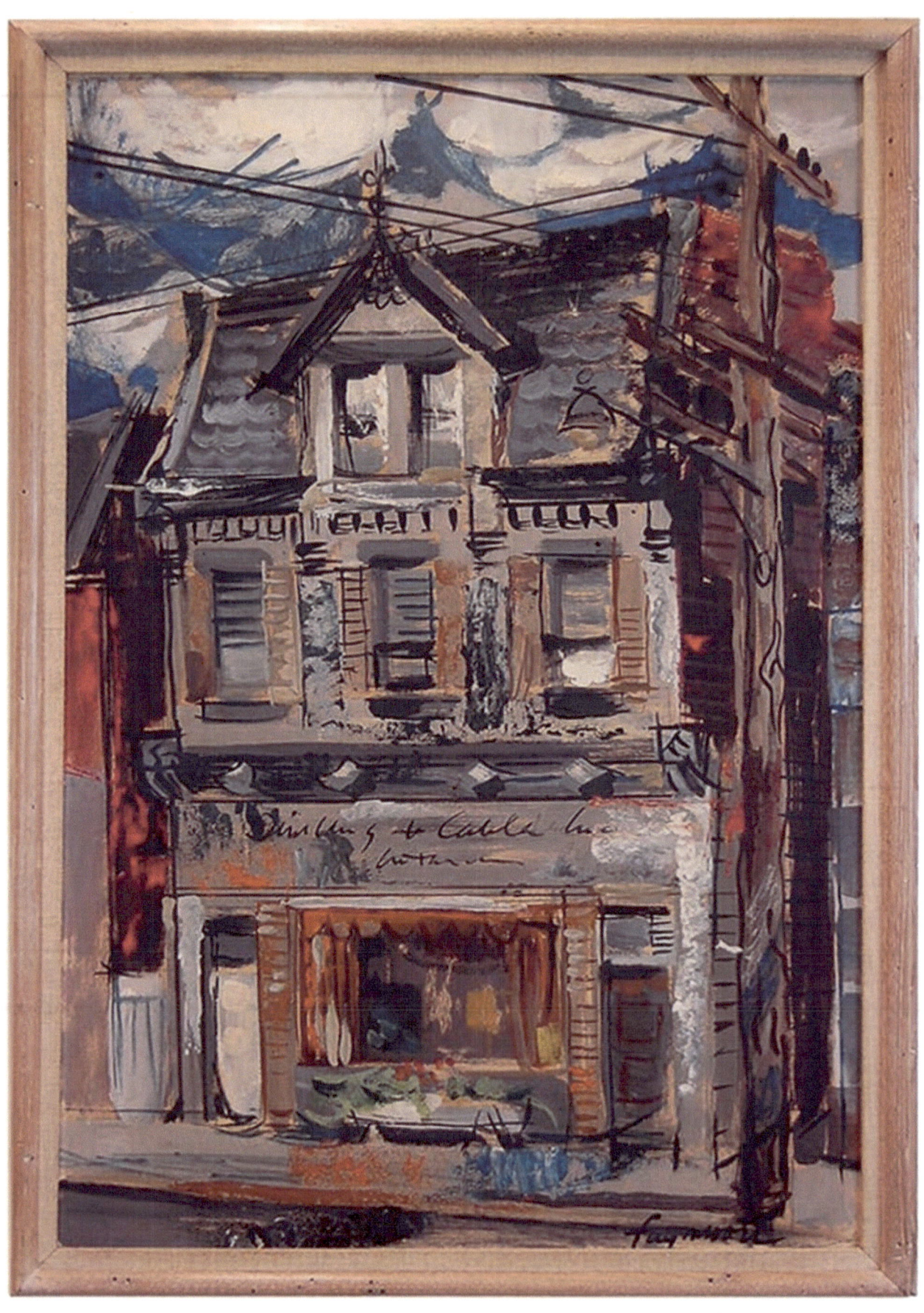

The painting was done in the 1960s by artist Fay Moore and is the earliest depiction of 5522 Walnut St. I was able to uncover. We clearly see the mansard roof described by Emily Litz in 1890.

We see also there are doors on both the left and right, while in modern times - there is only one door in the center. We also see alleyways on either side of the building. The bricks on the building to the right are consistent with the Shadyside Theater. However, with the bricks on the left we can see the rightmost side of what was likely a house at the time with a slanted roof.

I am genuinely proud to say that this painting, as of writing this book, hangs in Kards Unlimited. The painting is home. Carrying the spirit and love of Dimling & Cable back to the halls and walls within which they laughed so many decades ago. Unfortunately I could find very little information on Fay Moore. I am deeply grateful for their contribution to this project.

Dr. A Daniel Kaufman

1946-1958

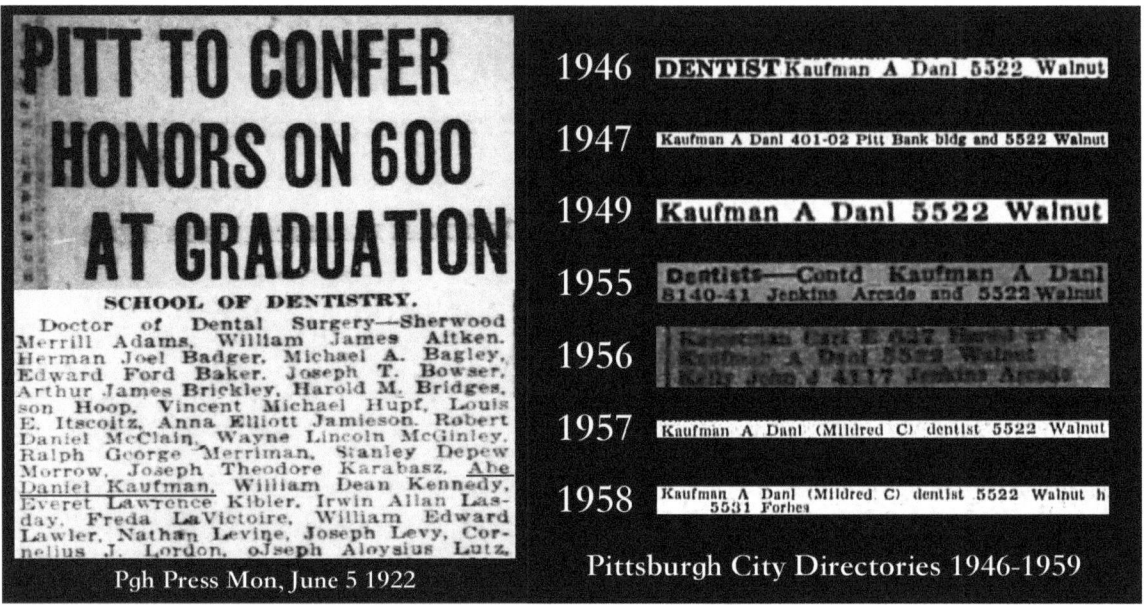

1946 DENTIST Kaufman A Danl 5522 Walnut

1947 Kaufman A Danl 401-02 Pitt Bank bldg and 5522 Walnut

1949 Kaufman A Danl 5522 Walnut

1955 Dentists—Contd Kaufman A Danl 8140-41 Jenkins Arcade and 5522 Walnut

1956

1957 Kaufman A Danl (Mildred C) dentist 5522 Walnut

1958 Kaufman A Danl (Mildred C) dentist 5522 Walnut h 5531 Forbes

Pittsburgh City Directories 1946-1959

PITT TO CONFER HONORS ON 600 AT GRADUATION

SCHOOL OF DENTISTRY.

Doctor of Dental Surgery—Sherwood Merrill Adams, William James Aitken. Herman Joel Badger, Michael A. Bagley, Edward Ford Baker, Joseph T. Bowser, Arthur James Brickley, Harold M. Bridges, son Hoop, Vincent Michael Hupf, Louis E. Itscoitz, Anna Elliott Jamieson, Robert Daniel McClain, Wayne Lincoln McGinley, Ralph George Merriman, Stanley Depew Morrow, Joseph Theodore Karabasz, Abe Daniel Kaufman, William Dean Kennedy, Everet Lawrence Kibler, Irwin Allan Lasday, Freda LaVictoire, William Edward Lawler, Nathan Levine, Joseph Levy, Cornelius J. Lordon, oJseph Aloysius Lutz,

Pgh Press Mon, June 5 1922

As the Benzenhoefer barbershop beauty parlor days come to a close we welcome Dr. Abe Daniel Kaufman. A 1922 graduate from the University of Pittsburgh dental school, Dr. Kaufman opened his own office at 5522 Walnut St. where he would maintain his private practice for at least 13 years.

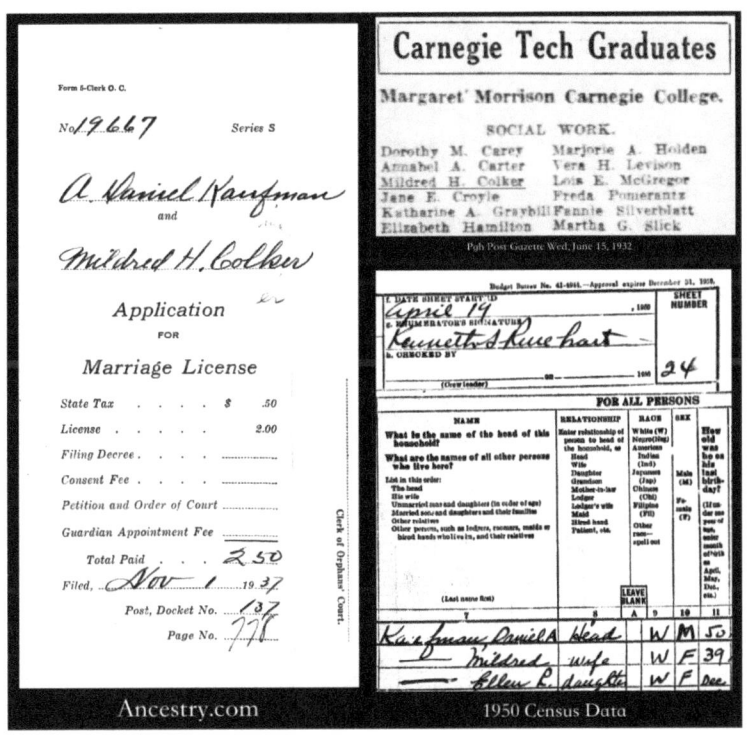

In 1937 Kaufman married Mildred Colker, a 1932 graduate from Margaret Morrison Carnegie College for Social Work. In December of 1949 they had a daughter named Ellen.

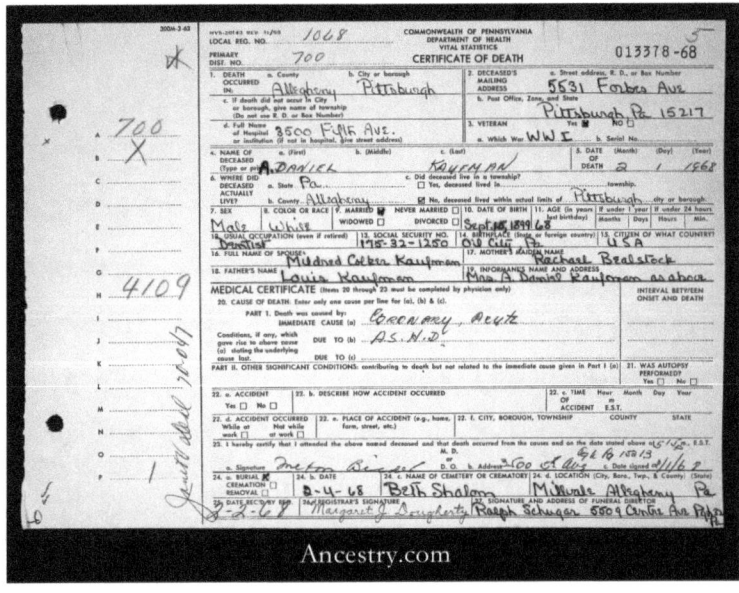

Kaufman died in 1968 and from his death certificate we learn that he was a veteran of WWI.

The Village Treat Shop

1962 - 1964

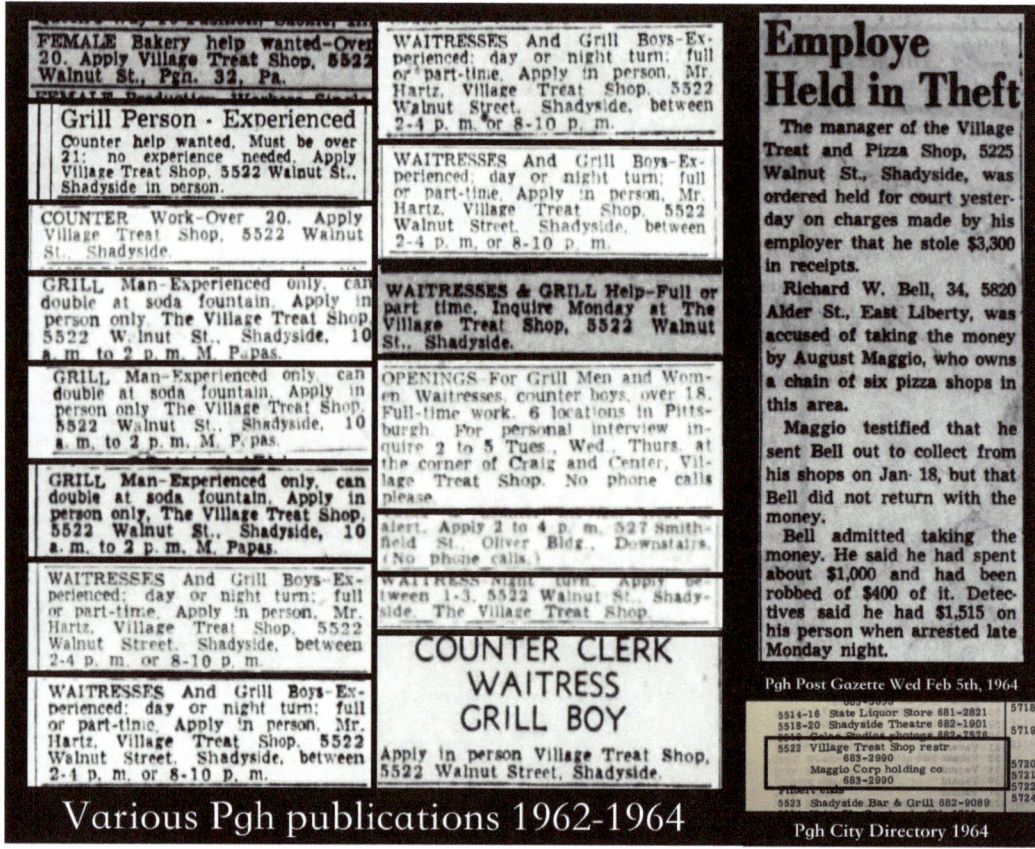

Various Pgh publications 1962-1964

The Village Treat shop isn't something I can say much about. In 1964 the manager robbed the store of $3,300 and was soon caught. And from these ads we can infer that it was a classic soda fountain joint with a grill that existed as a business at 5522 Walnut St at least from 1962-1964, and they were always hiring.

Papa Joe's

1964 - 1974

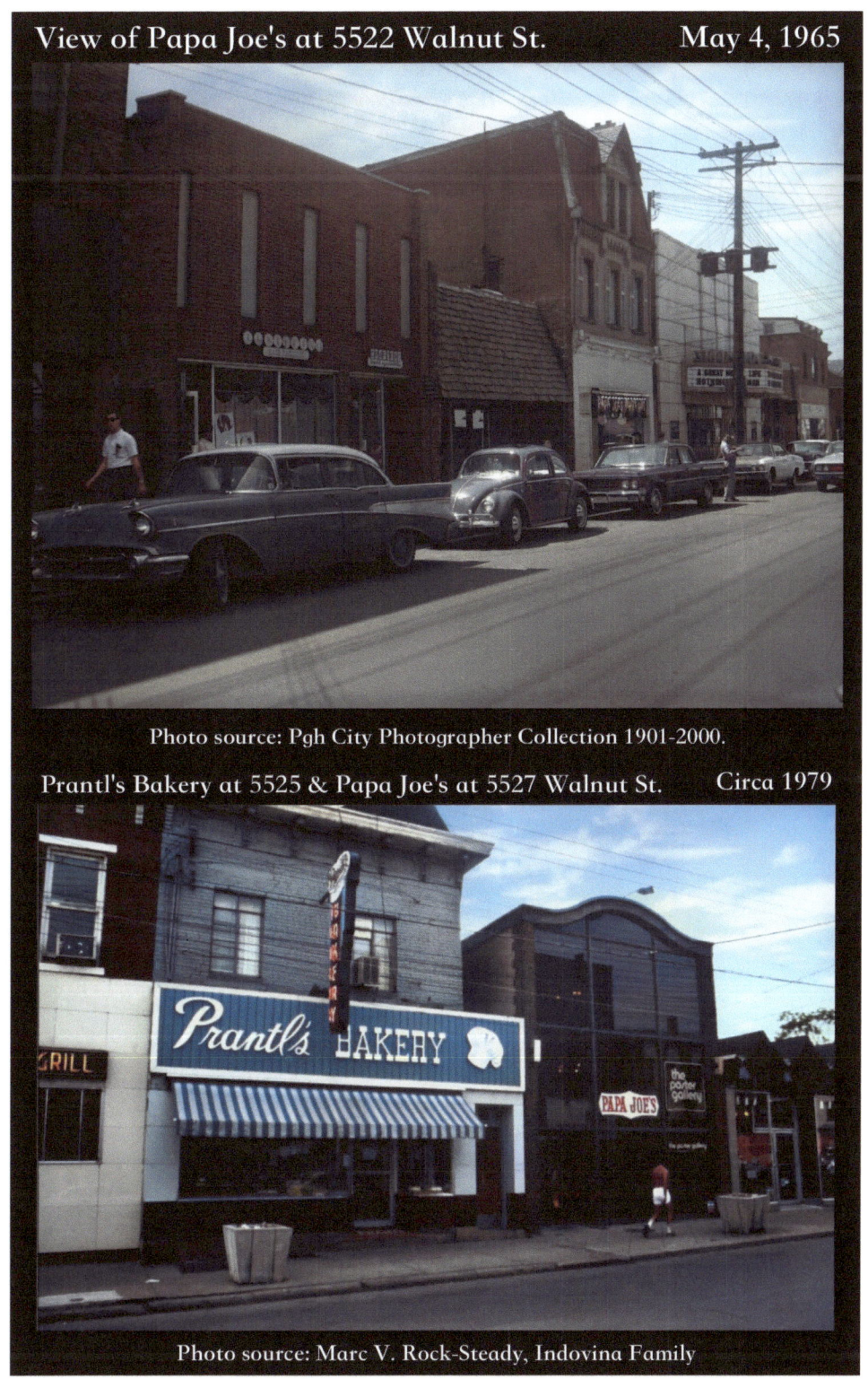

View of Papa Joe's at 5522 Walnut St.   May 4, 1965

Photo source: Pgh City Photographer Collection 1901-2000.

Prantl's Bakery at 5525 & Papa Joe's at 5527 Walnut St.   Circa 1979

Photo source: Marc V. Rock-Steady, Indovina Family

Originally located at the corner of Ivy and Walnut St. Papa Joe's moved to 5522 in 1964. At which point Joe's daughter, Jean Cohen was the owner.

I am not entirely certain where the name "White Hut" comes from. Through discussions in the Friends from Shadyside Facebook group the general consensus is that they may have been capitalizing on the already established "White Castle" and "White Hut" names. But also, and more likely, could simply be referring to a "white coffee," which was just a coffee with a bit of cream.

Papa Joe's White Hut   1965

Photo source: Ancestry.com, Benzenhoefer family home

What I love about these two photos is how much of this building has changed when comparing it to the Fay Moore painting. The alleyway has been bricked shut. However upon examination of the side of 5522, the memory of the neighbor's slanted roof and the apartment door remain.

Either way we can tell from this photo that sometime in the late 1960s they shortened the name, simply, to Papa Joe's.

Papa Joe's, The Shadyside Theater and State Store   July 1971

Photo source: Carnegie Library of Pittsburgh Photo Archives

In 1974 Papa Joe's moved to 5527 Walnut St. where its name remained until 1984 when Jean's daughter Pam Cohen and Pam's partner Gail Klingensmith take over ownership and change the name to Pamela's, making it the second Pamela's location after their first opened in Squirrel Hill in 1980.

Tavern in Castle Shannon 7:3
563-5983, 881-9842.
WAITRESS/waiter--apply in
person. PAPA JOE'S, 5527
Walnut St. in Shadyside.   SA
BOYS or GIRLS in Penn   pa
Hills, area 11, yrs old or co
COOK—Short Order, Exp,
apply in person, Papa Joe's
5527 Walnut, Shadyside.
1981 Post Gazette Ads

45

Adam's Rib Room

1976

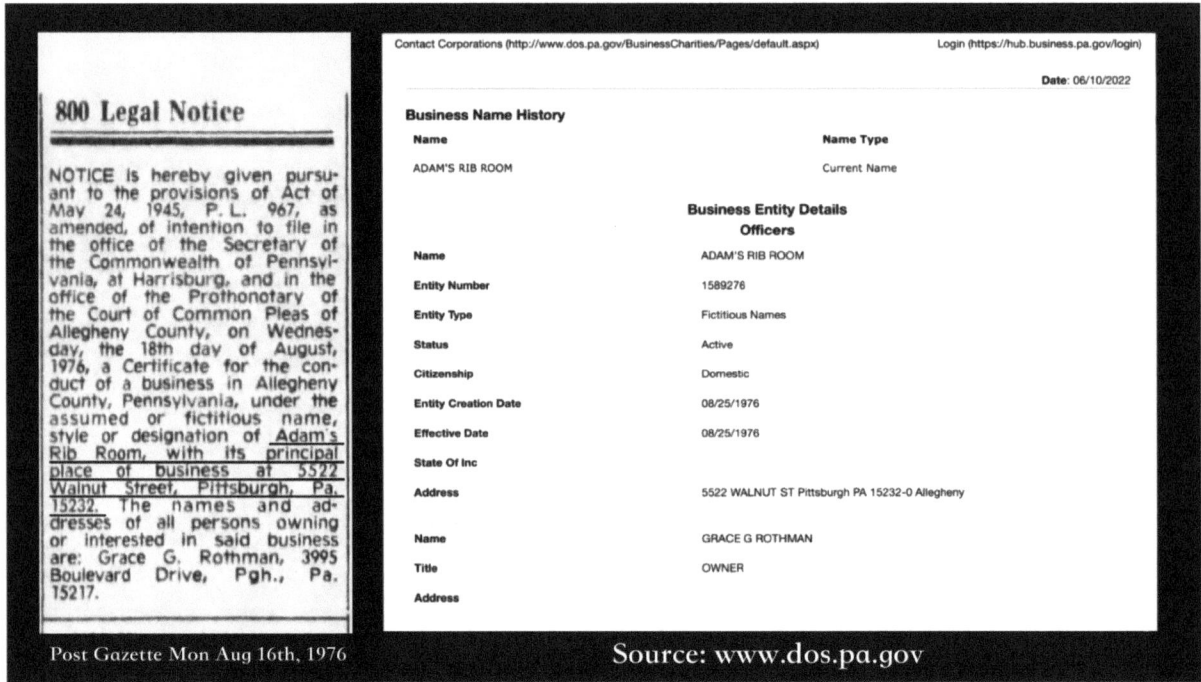

One of my favorite finds is Adam's Rib Room. A fictitious name for a fictitious company that opened at 5522 Walnut St in 1976. It's a favorite because everytime I go asking people about it they simply tell me, "that's when the mob owned the Hollywood Social Club, so I'd leave it alone..."

Either way I was able to uncover nothing besides these two sources.

The Hollywood Social Club

1948 - 1982

Source: Friends of Shadyside Facebook group

Exactly when ownership transferred from the Benzenhoefers to Blandi was a detail I was unable to uncover. Nonetheless it is clear that in 1948 restaurateur Frank Blandi set out to create the Hollywood Social Club.

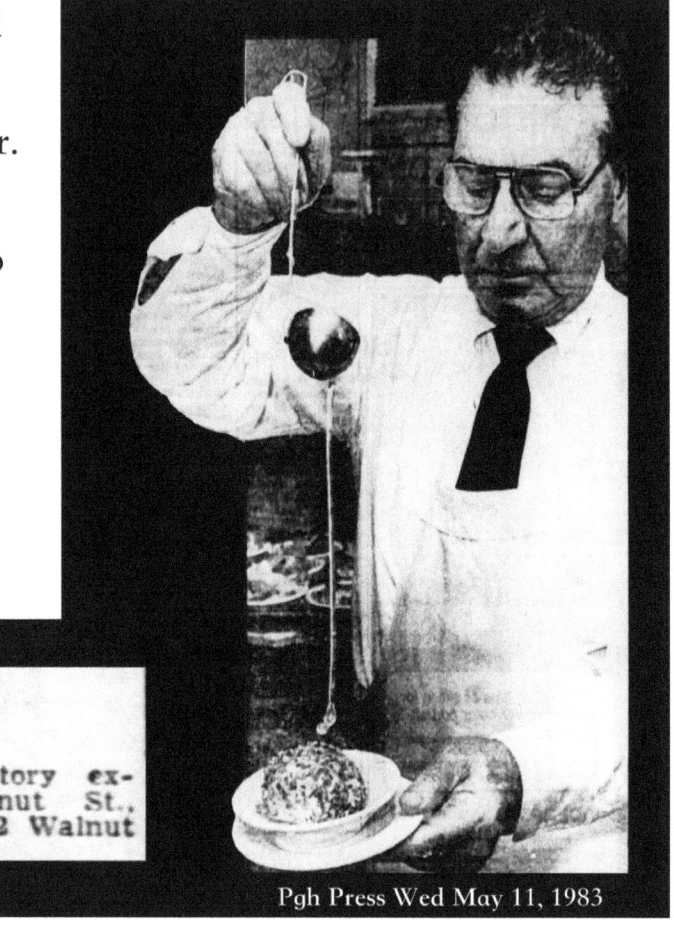

Pgh Press Wed May 11, 1983

Unsurpassed anywhere in the city The Hollywood Social Club would draw in unbelievable decades of celebrity sightings, endless evenings of jazz, the best food Pittsburgh has ever tasted and ... the mob.

Newspaper clippings from across multiple archives plus the narrative histories of members from the Friends from Shadyside Facebook group paint an intriguing picture of what this club may have been like.

The club experienced a few burglaries over the years. The first of which happened only a few months after the club had begun being built. Apparently a workman had left a "ladder leaning against the building" ltimately stealing $281. Flynn, apparently too drunk to realize, had left his wallet at the scene. When police finally found him - he admitted to the robbery and also to drinking $101 of the $281 he stole.

In 1951 they were burglarized of $317 cash and liquor valued at $200.

Then in 1959 they were robbed of $175 cash and $200 booze. On this date orphan Bernadette received her first beauty treatment.

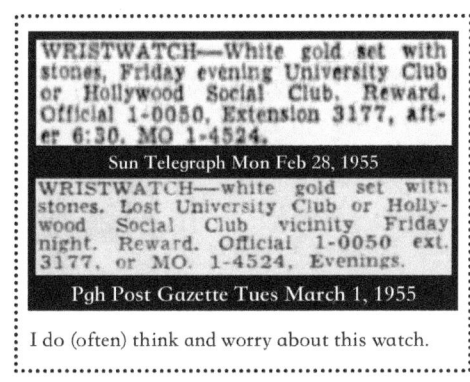

I do (often) think and worry about this watch.

Shadyside Fire Threatens Club

Fire broke out in the heart of the Shadyside business district yesterday afternoon, threatening a club, an interior decorating firm and a dentist's office in one building.

Only slight damage to the two-story structure at 5522 Walnut St. was reported by Fire Capt. Harold H. Huckestein, however.

The flames started in a ground-level incinerator, at the rear, belonging to the Hollywood Social Club on the second floor. Sharing the same address are Dimling & Cable Inc. and the offices of Dr. D. A. Kaufman, both on the first floor.

Pgh Press Sun Sept 23, 1956

Shadyside Club Fire Costs $500

A small fire which broke out in the kitchen of the Hollywood Social Club, 5522 Walnut Street, Shadyside, shortly after noon yesterday caused about $500 damage to the private club, according to police.

Joseph Cook, the chef, told police the fire started as he was taking a roast out of one of the ovens shortly after noon. An employe, Frances Puchtlo suffered minor burns on the right hand and was treated at the scene, police said.

Pgh Post Gazette Mon April 11, 1960

Bridge Director Honored

Club Members Pay Tribute At Farewell Dinner

Miss Claire Tiernan and her sister, Mary, came to Pittsburgh in 1927, the last time the Pirates won the pennant, and they are now leaving Pittsburgh.

Whether this is significant or not, nobody knows, but last night at the Hollywood Social Club the club's new bridge director, Charles L. DiFrancesco, mentioned Miss Claire Tiernan in connection with baseball.

Job Is Thankless

"Miss Tiernan directed the duplicate bridge games here for 11 years," he said, "and a bridge director is like a baseball umpire. She must be patient, unbiased and have a sense of humor. Her job is thankless."

Claire, left, and Mary Tiernan admire farewell gift.

Pgh Post Gazette Fri Sept 9 1960

The club had at least two fires. The first in 1956 and the second in 1960.

A decade of bridge games were played at the club's tables.

It is, however, the 1961 and 1964 Golden Anniversary announcements that I am taken by. For I wish to be so lucky as to love and be loved for such a period of time. Congratulations to both the DiNardos and the Perinos on their 50th wedding anniversaries.

East End Pair Dinner Guests

Mr. and Mrs. Gennero Perrino, of 162 Luna St., East End, will celebrate their 50th wedding anniversary today with a dinner at the Hollywood Social Club.

The couple has two sons, John, of Greentree, and Jerry, of Mt. Lebanon; one daughter, Mrs. Rose Giardina, of East End, and nine grandchildren.

Pgh Press Sun Feb 9, 1964

Couple to Mark Golden Wedding

Pasquale and Mary DiNardo, 128 Auburn St., East Liberty, will observe their 50th wedding anniversary on Thursday with a family dinner at the Hollywood Social Club, Shadyside.

The couple has two children, Mrs. Teresa Perino, Pasquale Jr., and eight grandchildren.

Pgh Post Gazette Sun May 21, 1961

Festival to Depict City's Early Days

Pittsburgh's early days will be depicted in the annual Shadyside Spring Festival and Street Fair Monday through Saturday.

Proceeds will go into a college scholarship fund for Shadyside youth. It is sponsored by Shadyside Chamber of Commerce.

A parade featuring dress popular at the turn of the century will be held Friday at 8 p. m. Prizes will be awarded.

A TREASURE HUNT for $50 in silver supplied by Shadyside merchants will begin Monday. Clues will be supplied at headquarters, Walnut and Ivy Sts.

A Children's party will be held in Hollywood Social Club on Walnut St. Thursday from 4:30 to 6 p. m.

A dog show will be held Friday at 7:30 p. m. at Shadyside Shopping Center. An entry fee of 25 cents will go to the scholarship fund.

A CARNIVAL AIR will prevail on Walnut St. Saturday with a midway, refreshments and a Dixieland band on hand.

A king and queen will be crowned following a fashion show late Saturday.

Wallet Stolen

Alex Johns of 12 E. Main St., Carnegie, told police his wallet containing $6 was stolen by a pickpocket while he was standing at the Penn Ave. and Stanwix St. trolley stop yesterday.

FOR FAIR: Mayor Lawrence getting an invitation to the Shadyside Spring Festival and Street Fair next week from Mrs. A. F. Kittell and Mrs. Paul E. Olson, co-chairmen. He said he'll be there.
Sun-Telegraph Photo by Morris Berman

Shadyside Poster Artists Are Selected

Work to Adorn Store Windows For Festive Week

The Shadyside Chamber of Commerce yesterday named the three winners in a poster contest in which seventh and eighth graders at Liberty School drew advertising for the Shadyside Street Fair.

Saturday, Shadyside merchants will shut up shop and turn Walnut Street into a carnival with games and refreshments, models and music.

Thursday's schedule calls for a kiddie's party from 4:30 to 6 p. m. at the Hollywood Social Club. Friday merchants and many customers will dress in "Gay Nineties" costumes.

Pgh Sun Telegraph Fri June 7, 1957

Pgh Post Gazette Thurs June 6, 1957

Now here is where we change it up and begin to see Walnut St from new perspectives. Here is where stories told in news clippings merge with photography to bring the past momentarily into the relative present.

Here in 1957, closing out our decade, we catch an uncanny and visceral glimpse of that change. The Hollywood Social Club throws a children's party during The Shadyside Chamber of Commerce festival on Walnut St. A festival captured across several images by photographer W. Eugene Smith.

Scan QR code to be taken to Shadyside Chamber of Commerce Spring Festival and Street Fair 1957!

Shadyside Chamber of Commerce Festival 1957

View from Mobile Gas Station at 5416 Walnut St.   1957

Shadyside Chamber of Commerce Festival   Photographer W. Eugene Smith

SW View from Bellefonte and Walnut St.   1957

Shadyside Chamber of Commerce Festival   Photographer W. Eugene Smith

View of 5411 Walnut St.   1957

Shadyside Chamber of Commerce Festival   Photographer W. Eugene Smith

Mobile Gas Station at 5416 Walnut St.   1957

Shadyside Chamber of Commerce Festival   Photographer W. Eugene Smith

Girl Leaning on a Parking Meter   1957

Shadyside Chamber of Commerce Festival   Photographer W. Eugene Smith

Photographer W. Eugene Smith

Survey Finds Gambling, Girls In After-Hours Spots
Money's All You Need To Drink In Some Clubs

Clubs violating the law against serving non-members, on the basis of The Press survey, included:

Almono Club, 518 Court Pl.; Club 30, 136 Sixth St. (second floor); Young Men's Thinking Club (second floor), 3418 Forbes Ave., Oakland; Aloysius Section Two, 5703 Penn Ave. (second floor), East Liberty; Hollywood Social Club, 5522 Walnut St. (second floor), Shadyside; Lyric Club, 5711 Ellsworth Ave., East Liberty; and South Pacific Club, 2943-45 Penn Ave.

Of these, Almono, Young Men's, Aloysius and Club 30 served guests long after the designated cut-off time of 3 a. m.

(The upstairs at 136 Sixth St. has an interesting history, of afterhour club activity.

rooms were occupied by the

.ce Lt. Allen Carnahan was wounded with his service revolver while at the bar at 6 a. m. He resigned from the force after the shooting, which involved a woman companion, Shirley Cavanaugh.

Warning ignored at Hollywood Social Club.

Pgh Press Sun Dec 25, 1960

Club Waives LCB Hearing

The Hollywood Social Club, 5522 Walnut St., Shadyside, waived a hearing scheduled here today before a State Liquor Control Board (LCB) examiner.

The club in effect was pleading no defense to LCB citations for sales to non-members and after-hours sales.

The club was one of seven singled out as a liquor-law violator by reporters for The Press after touring the after-hours spots to gather evidence for an article published last Dec. 25.

Pgh Press Tues May 2, 1961

The Hollywood in Shadyside
Liquor Board Suspends Social Club's License

The state Liquor Control Board yesterday suspended the license of the Hollywood Social Club of Allegheny County, one of the most popular gathering places in the Shadyside night life belt.

Eight charges are listed in the board's complaint against the club at 5522 Walnut St. The license suspension begins July 15 and is effective for 50 days "and thereafter until conditions are corrected."

However, a licensee has the option of either closing during the suspension term or paying a fine of $10 for each day. The board may either accept or reject the fine payment.

Says Shortage in Income

The board's bill of particulars alleges that the club: Failed to adhere to by-laws; failed to maintain records in conformity with board regulations; failed to keep for a period of at least two years complete and truthful records.

Further, the board charges that there was an unexplained shortage in the club's reported cash income.

The suspension order goes on to cite the club for admitting persons to membership without written application, investigation and ballot. It also asserts employes were permitted to serve and collect for food sold by a concessionaire.

Cited Over Dues

Furthermore, the club is cited for failing to charge and collect dues from members, and failing to present separate checks for food and alcoholic beverages served to members.

Other liquor license suspensions in the county were ordered for:

James R. Mann, McKees Rocks; 20 days, sales after hours; permitted gambling.

Ralph J. Blakeley and Martha Misencik, operators of the Shamrock Cafe, 1519 Penn Ave., Strip District, 10 days. In this case, the board cited the fact that last January Blakeley pleaded guilty in Federal Court here to failure to obtain a $50 wagering tax stamp.

Pgh Post Gazette Thurs July 2, 1964

In 1960 The Hollywood Social Club got busted for selling booze, after hours, to non-members. In 1961 they pleaded no defense. In 1964 they got their license suspended.

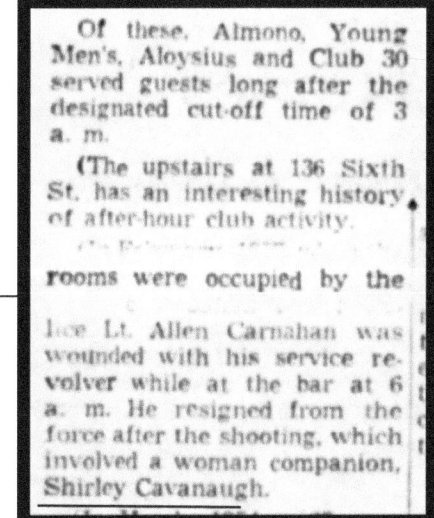

Of these, Almono, Young Men's, Aloysius and Club 30 served guests long after the designated cut-off time of 3 a. m.

(The upstairs at 136 Sixth St. has an interesting history, of after-hour club activity.

rooms were occupied by the

.ce Lt. Allen Carnahan was wounded with his service revolver while at the bar at 6 a. m. He resigned from the force after the shooting, which involved a woman companion, Shirley Cavanaugh.

Here, however, is a coincidence hard to ignore. In the article "Money's All You Need To Drink In Some Clubs" a familiar name and story leapt out at me... Grandma Shirley... The reason why I began doing research in the first place.

But that's not what the Hollywood Social Club was truly about was it? The golden anniversaries, the robberies, the children's party and bridge; all binding around the edge of a quilt. The fringe momentary stitches that wander the borders around the larger picture.

This was not the Benzenhoefer's Walnut St. That much is certain. This was Walnut St. in the 1960s. Musical culture and barefooted poet hippies are playing bongos at the coffee shops.

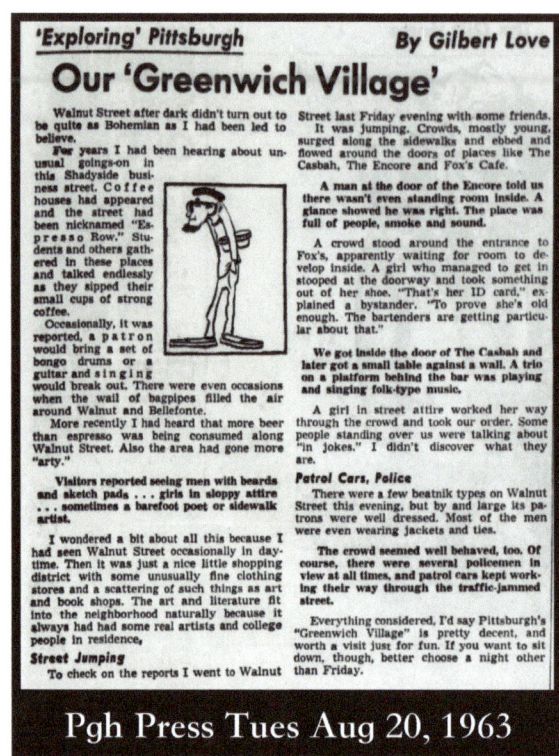

Pgh Press Tues Aug 20, 1963

Harold Betters records Live at The Encore, David & Anthony record Walnut St. Live at The Casbah.

As for us... Well, we cruise into 1965 in style...

"Walnut Street at Night"   May 1965

Photo source: Carnegie Library of Pittsburgh Photo Archives   Photographer: Bill Foster

Night, Walnut St. Laughter and light blare from the Shadyside Theater.

Like moths to beautiful moonlight we are carried by the sounds of jazz and scents of Devonshires down the block. Arriving at a speakeasy alleyway we climb an "Everest of stairs" until we come upon a door marked "Members Only."

But no sweat right? Remember if you got the money it's fine...

Warning ignored at Hollywood Social Club.

We ring the buzzer and head inside The Hollywood Social Club. Our coats are checked. Now a walk through the crowd reveals some familiar faces...

Ric Maroni, the former trumpet player in Johnny Costa's old band, now has his own combo at the Escapade on Monday nights and the Hollywood Social Club on Saturdays. It includes Bob Kress on bass, Danny Varlotto on drums and Ronnie Bickel, the son of Bill Bickel, the long-time organist (now retired) at Johnny Laughlin's Shamrock Room, on the piano. . . . Connie Lauar has moved her ticket agency from the Penn-Sheraton Hotel, where it was located for four years, to the Peerless-Willoughby Camera Store at 431 Smithfield Street. The Midtown Ticket Agency will identify it henceforth.

Not the least of which; upon a Saturday night you might hear the wondrous trumpet stylings of Rick Maroni.

★ ★ ★

After wearing out two of the original Broadway cast albums of "Fiddler On the Roof," Gert and Bill Mazefsky, the Civic Light Opera Company's publicity director, are finally going to see the show itself in New York this week-end. . . . The Lenny Litmans have a 20th wedding anniversary coming up on December 28. . . . Roland King has resigned as the film editor at Channel 2. . . . The Holiday House's John Bertera was the dinner host to his outgoing star, Kay Starr, and his incoming headliner, Gail Martin, at the Hollywood Social Club on Sunday night.

★ ★ ★

The 22 - year - old singing daughter of Dean Martin, of Steubenville, O., where she was born, is the current headliner at the Holiday House and will be through December 17. Miss Martin, a Reprise Record artist, was featured on her father's summer replacement television show this year with Vic Damone. The Day Brothers, a comedy team, are at the Holiday House, too.

GAIL MARTIN

Or catch the golden trills of Gail Martin's Sunday night serenade.

Birth of cool

After World War II, the place really changed. One sign of its transformation came on a cold spring morning in the late 1950s. Steve Snow, who grew up near Walnut Street and brokered real estate deals there, remembers the moment clearly.

His phone rang at 3 a.m. "This is Orson Welles," said the voice on the other end of the line. "I am coming to Pittsburgh." Welles asked Snow, an old prep school classmate in Illinois, to meet him the next night.

"What are you going to do with me?" Welles asked.

Snow said, "I am going to take you to Walnut Street."

At the time, the street was gaining a reputation as a hot night spot. Welles and Snow had their choice of nightclubs and restaurants.

They started with a few drinks at the Fox's Cafe, a bar at the corner of Walnut and Bellefonte streets. Later, they walked to the Hollywood Social Club. To get in, they had to squeeze down a side alley, walk several flights and hit a buzzer on the third floor.

Inside, the after-hours club featured a bar that stretched from one end of the room to the other. A back room was full of people, including comedian Henny Youngman. Welles and Youngman spent a few minutes talking and exchanging one-liners. Welles and Snow stayed at the Hollywood Social Club until 5 a.m. or 6 a.m., with the actor catching an early-morning flight out of town.

In the late 1950s and early 1960s, celebrities, local politicians, athletes, attorneys and executives filled the street at night. Among the repeat visitors was comedian Bob Hope, who buzzed through in the 1960s and 1970s. People spotted him with friend Billy Conn, the Pittsburgh prizefighter. Conn would drive Hope around Pittsburgh and often end the night at the Hollywood Social Club.

Once, Ralph Colaizzi spotted Hope emerging from the alley at 8 a.m. Colaizzi owned the building. He didn't speculate on what kept the star so long.

Down the street, the Encore jazz club was playing host to musicians such as trumpet players Roy Eldridge and Yank Larson, trombone player Harold Betters and pianist Earl Hines. Today, Cozumel Mexicana and Victoria's Secret sit on the spot.

People lined up to get into the Encore, according to Carol Rosenbloom. "This wasn't just weekends. This was every night."

In the late 1960s, Willard Shiner opened the Gaslight, a three-story club-style place just off Walnut on Bellefonte that was controversial because of its nude paintings.

Nightclubs were not the only new arrivals. Fashion hit the street, too.

Pgh Post Gazette Sun Sept 26, 1999

Or perhaps it's your lucky night and you run into none other than Orson Welles. Who upon a 3a.m. visit to Pittsburgh called up his childhood prep school classmate Steve Snow, grumbling into the phone, "I'm coming to Pittsburgh, what will you do with me?" The answer no doubt being - "we're going to the Hollywood Social Club."

Orson Welles

Henny Youngman

Where that same night Henny Youngman sat crackin' jokes across the strings of his violin. Or you arrived one night where suddenly Billy Conn and Bob Hope stumble punch drunkenly past you in the cramped Hollywood Social Club Alleyway.

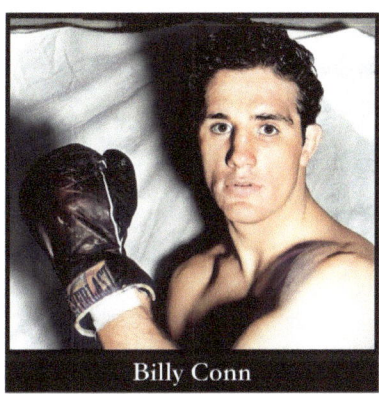
Billy Conn

Bob Hope

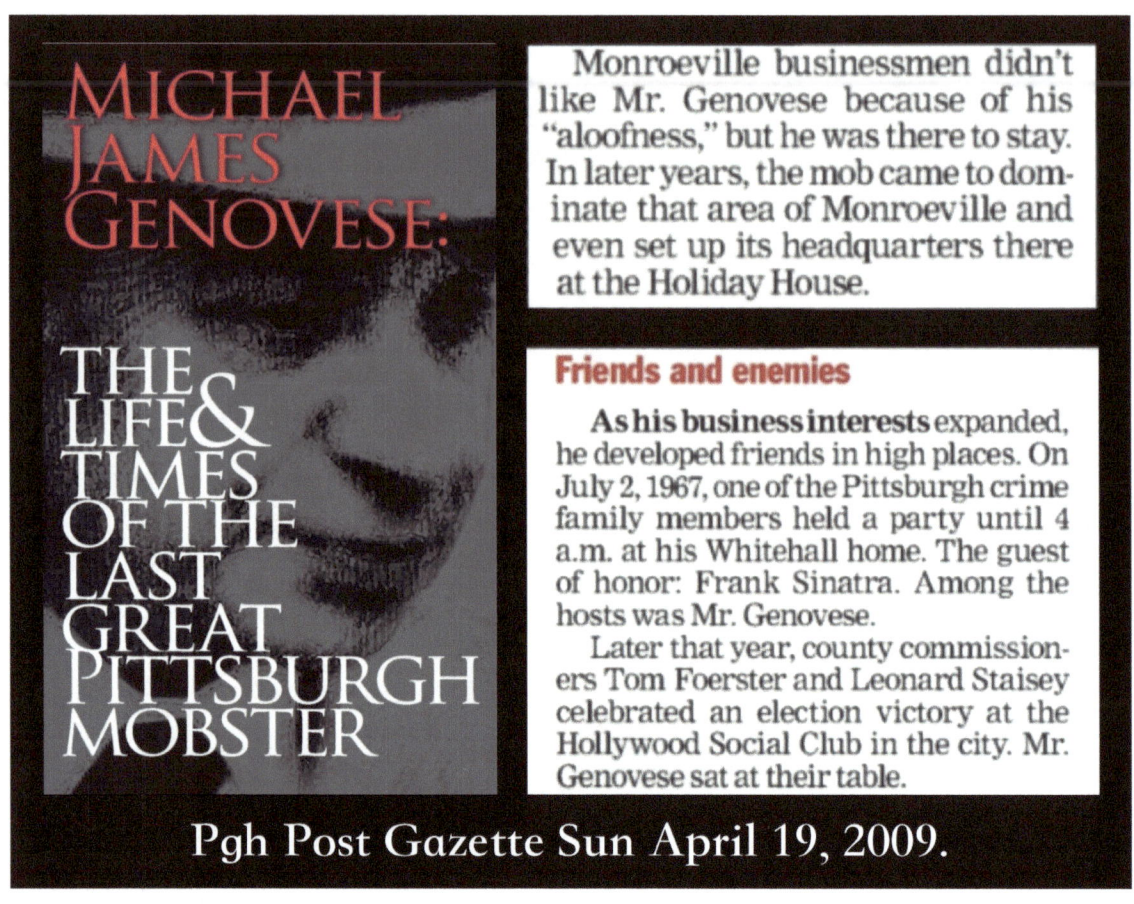

MICHAEL JAMES GENOVESE:

THE LIFE & TIMES OF THE LAST GREAT PITTSBURGH MOBSTER

Monroeville businessmen didn't like Mr. Genovese because of his "aloofness," but he was there to stay. In later years, the mob came to dominate that area of Monroeville and even set up its headquarters there at the Holiday House.

Friends and enemies

As his business interests expanded, he developed friends in high places. On July 2, 1967, one of the Pittsburgh crime family members held a party until 4 a.m. at his Whitehall home. The guest of honor: Frank Sinatra. Among the hosts was Mr. Genovese.

Later that year, county commissioners Tom Foerster and Leonard Staisey celebrated an election victory at the Hollywood Social Club in the city. Mr. Genovese sat at their table.

Pgh Post Gazette Sun April 19, 2009.

While there does seem to be some sort of connection between the Pittsburgh Mafia and The Hollywood Social Club I could find very little to support this. Whether it is true or not I can't say. I can only say, with this one reference, that Michael James Genovese "The Last Great Pittsburgh Mobster" was headquartered at the Holiday House in Monroeville and would often be seen having dinner with some fairly important people at the Hollywood Social Club.

No matter who you'd run into - one thing was certain, The Hollywood Social Club, was really about the food.

While Frank Blandi may have invented the Devonshire, he perfected the Deviled Crab. Or at least that's the way Patricia Goodwin of Las Vegas remembers it...

Arlene Burnett's Kitchen Mailbox in the Cook's Corner section of the Post-Gazette in 2004. A full 22 years after the club's closure. Patricia casts a long shot hoping someone out there might still have the recipe for it.

And you know what?

Someone did...

Shadyside club drew celebs, request for its deviled crab

Bob Hope never left Pittsburgh without stopping in for a nightcap. Chubby Checker "twisted" for a plate of veal scaloppine. "Old Blue Eyes" and Sammy Davis, Jr. visited on more than one occasion.

From 1956 to the mid-'70s, the Hollywood Social Club on Walnut Street in Shadyside was one of the hottest night spots in Pittsburgh.

"Pittsburgh Steelers owner Art Rooney, local celebrities and athletes would stop in for dinner," said owner Chuck DiNardo. "We were known for our Devonshire sandwiches (we served about 1,000 a week) and deviled crab."

Which brings us to Patricia Goodwin of Las Vegas, who remembers the Hollywood Social Club's deviled crab: "I lived in Pittsburgh from birth through the '50s. I would frequent the Hollywood Social Club. On the menu was deviled crab, and to this day I think about it. Would any of your readers have the recipe?"

Mr. DiNardo willingly gave us the recipe, and we're delighted he did; this dish is outstanding.

HOLLYWOOD SOCIAL CLUB DEVILED CRAB
PG tested

- ½ cup half-and-half
- 1 to 1½ teaspoons dry mustard
- A few dashes Worcestershire sauce
- Salt and pepper to taste
- 6 slices white bread, crusts removed and cubed
- 1 pound lump crab meat
- Fresh bread crumbs, about ¼ cup
- About ¼ to ¼ cup melted butter, plus more for coating the casserole dish or ramekins

Preheat oven to 400 degrees. Butter the inside of a 1-quart casserole dish or four 7-ounce ramekins (we used a casserole dish). Place the half-and-half in a medium-size bowl. Stir in the mustard, Worcestershire sauce and salt and pepper.

Add the bread cubes and crab, and gently mix until all ingredients are incorporated.

Place the crab mixture in casserole dish or ramekins. Sprinkle bread crumbs over the crab mixture. Drizzle about ¼ cup of melted butter over mixture.

Bake in a 350-degree oven for 20 to 25 minutes.

Broil for about 30 seconds or until crumbs are golden brown. Drizzle 1 to 2 tablespoons of melted butter over the crumbs.

A note from Mr. DiNardo: "We would place the crab dish under an open flame until the bread crumbs turned golden brown. Then we would drizzle additional melted butter over crumbs and serve. This recipe is also good for stuffing flounder."

Pgh Post Gazette Thurs June 22, 2006

Two years later, thanks to owner Chuck DiNardo, the Post-Gazette not only ran the recipe in response to Goodwin's request but also took that time to namedrop Chubby Checker, Art Rooney, Sammy Davis Jr. and Frank Sinatra as people you might find hanging out some random night at The Hollywood Social Club.

Correction

Last week's recipe for the Hollywood Social Club's Deviled Crab recipe incorrectly said to preheat the oven to 400 degrees. The correct temperature is 350 degrees.

Pgh Post Gazette Thurs July 6, 2006

Chubby Checker

Art Rooney

Sammy Davis Jr.

Frank Sinatra

Every Cloud Has a Dynamic Lining or Time to Embrace Change, Barbara.

Some people are happy with the same old thing

Some people don't like change.

They get over it most of the time, but they certainly do squeal a lot before they adjust.

Maybe you don't fit into this category, but I do. I tend to like things to remain the same as long as possible. A great deal of the reluctance to accept change has to do with age.

I admit it. I'm older and I don't like feeling unsettled.

BARBARA CLOUD,

Would Shadyside ever be the same without its Hollywood Social Club? And what about the theaters we've lost? I still mourn the fact movie houses are now on the outskirts of the city or in malls. And the original Nixon Theater being torn down for the Alcoa Building, then the second Nixon giving way on Liberty Avenue.

We will adjust to the loss of Horne's. But hold onto your memories. They are yours to keep forever.

Nobody can change that.

Pgh Post Gazette Tues May 10, 1994

In the 1994 article "Some people are happy with the same old thing," Barbara Cloud expresses an emotional state of being we can all relate to; a fear of, and so reluctance to, change. A longing to remain comfortably cradled within the arms of familiarity.

Asking ourselves, how could the present moment be meaningful without the past? And what about the future? Will this moment have been meaningful to us?

Would Shadyside find the same meaning now that the Hollywood Social Club is gone? Now that the theaters have disappeared?

No.

Walnut St. has always reflected the human experience. An experience best described as seasonal. Clinging to spring or fall will not impede the peak arrivals of summer and winter. But upon their arrival, we would not be prepared. Being sticky with the past ensures anxiety of the present and dread of the future.

So we too must change. With the seasons, we must fall. With the years, we must brush aside the leaves. With the decades we too must emerge like blossoms beneath so much snow.

As the 1960s rolled into the 1970s, Walnut St changed further and became known for its Arts Festival, music scene and eateries.

Shadyside Arts Festival 1975
Photographer: Tom Doyle

The Clay Place and The Lemon Tree Shop   Late 1970s

Photo source: Carnegie Library of Pittsburgh Photo Archives   (demolished 1987)

The Lemon Tree Shop and Clay place stand beautifully at Ivy and Walnut. The Music Emporium, Call Me Mister, Yogurt Works and Mardi Gras sit near the corner of Bellefonte and Walnut.

Call me Mister, The Music Emporium, Yogurt Works, Mardi Gras   Late 1970s

Photo source: Carnegie Library of Pittsburgh   Corner of Bellefonte and Walnut St.

And Kards Unlimited, isn't where you think it is...

Kards Unlimited

1974 - Present Day

Post Gazette December 1976 ad

Google 2022 Street View

Photo source: Carnegie Library of Pittsburgh Photo Archives   Photographer Richard J. Dadowski

Originally a Hallmark store, Kards Unlimited first opened its doors in 1957 at 5513 Walnut St. where it would remain until 1974.

Regardless of its location the ethos remained the same. Be tasteful, be quirky, be fun, entertain, spread laughter, enliven the holiday spirit, be a safe and creative space for people to visit and shop for new aspects of themselves.

1947 CMU Yearbook Photo

And few knew this better than Clara Herron...

Shopping with Polly
1927

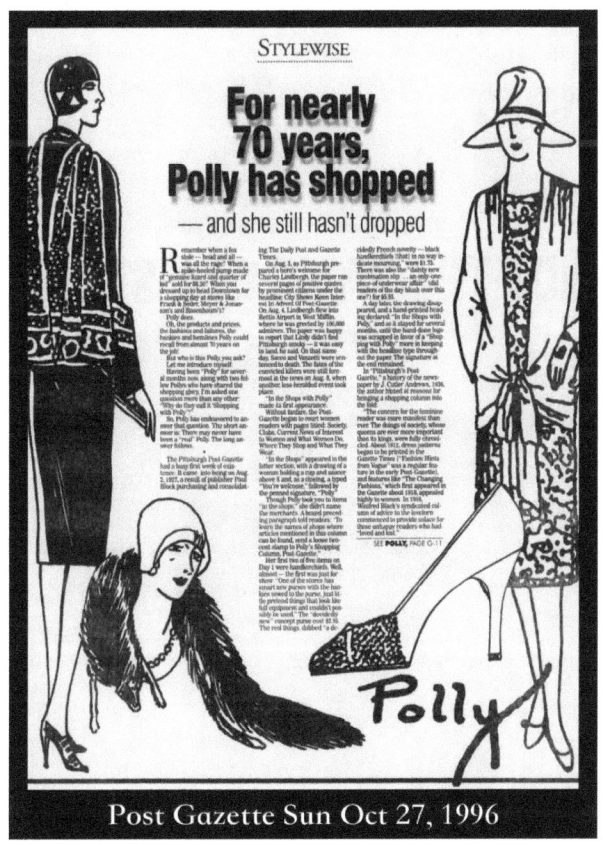

Post Gazette Sun Oct 27, 1996

Within the first week of the launch of the Pittsburgh Post Gazette, August 8, 1927 a column titled "In the Shops With Polly" began its run.

Originating as a column geared towards the "feminine reader," "In the Shops With Polly" was concerned with the quality and care put into specific products. Complete with a shopping list infused with comfort, fun and local eccentricity.

Since 1927 the nom de plume "Polly" was penned by a plethora of different journalists, but the Polly that concerns us most is Clara Herron.

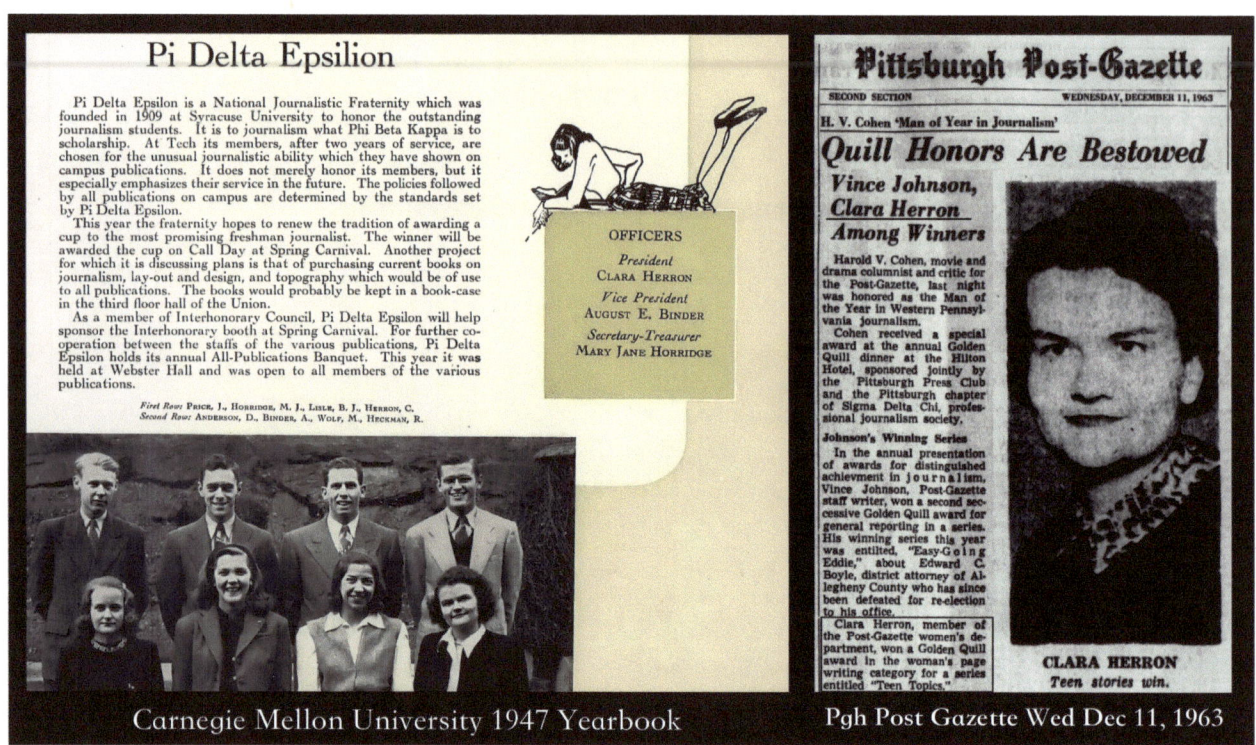

Carnegie Mellon University 1947 Yearbook

Pgh Post Gazette Wed Dec 11, 1963

President of Carnegie Mellon University's journalist fraternity Pi Delta Epsilon and Golden Quill award winner Clara Herron would write as Polly from 1954-1987.

And from 1974-1987 Clara frequently made certain her Polly columns included products from Kards Unlimited

Post Gazette Sun Oct 27, 1996

See Posters, Pots, Prints

Place to go for all the posters is Kards Unlimited, 5513 Walnut St., Shadyside. But Polly got the word that the store will move to a new location just across the street, 522 Walnut St., in a week or so. After the move, the store plans to expand its poster panorama and also include framed art works.

Thurs Aug 8. 1974

Shopping With Polly

Heavy Snows Warming Sale of Mushy Valentines

Bottled Love

Instead of a ship, you can get a heart in a hand-blown bottle for $2 at Kards Unlimited.

Or you can write original love thoughts in "pure" white ink on bright red stationery.

Fri Feb 10, 1978

Shopping with Polly

Doll Houses
Number Two

More Than Cards

Kards, Unlimited, Shadyside, is noted for its greetings from far lands, and from the cleverest creators on our shores.

It has a doll house we hear is spectacular. A tiny parcel post package . . . an outdoor rural mailbox, $3. That's 5522 Walnut St.

Fri Nov 18, 1977

Shopping With Polly

Fun Felicitations

Can't ignore the birthday bunch just because it's summer. To a fisherman, send a soft-art " Fat Mail" card that will make a splash — a fat, vinyl fish, with "Here's your Happy Birthday cod," written on attached luggage tag. To anyone, send Old Sol with the legend,"Happy Birthday, Sunshine!" For a sick-abed, or any good egg, send one stuffed, with text: "Keep Your Sunny Side Up!" With mailing envelope, $1.75 each.

Kards Unlimited, 5522 Walnut St.

Tues June 24, 1980

Polly Says

COVER ART done by Pauline Ellison for the paperback edition of Ursula LeGuin's "A Wizard of Earthsea" is a full-color illustration in a collection of posters, notecards and prints matted for framing. They're from The Bantam Gallery, new division of Bantam Books, and will arrive soon at Kards Unlimited, 5522 Walnut St., Shadyside.

Sat May 20, 1978

Shopping With Polly

Little Boxes

Tiny In-Tins, saying such things as "Stamps and Stuff," "Baubles, Bangles and Beads," "Junque" and "Pandora," $1, were so popular last year that they've spawned a crop of boxes just a bit bigger.

They're survival kits for golfers, tennis buffs, runners, dieters, cyclists and drinkers.

Each one costs $1.50. Instant chicken broth, a stick-on bandage, aspirin, a wash towelette, are found in tiny packets in each.

Then a tire patch is added for the cyclist, a tape measure for the dieter, salt tablets for the runner.

Kards Unlimited/ 5522 Walnut St./Shadyside/other stationers

Tues Feb 20, 1979

Shopping With Polly

Imagine this!

The Beatles 1983 Song Calendar, $6.95, adds 52 extra days to your year to help you crowd it all in. Beatle melodies "Eight Days a Week," "Help" and "Imagine," nine others are featured on pages headed by color illustrations first seen on greeting cards.

Important Beatle dates are identified each month, and there are quotes from John Lennon and Paul McCartney.

Kards Unlimited,
5522 Walnut St.,
Shadyside;
University Bookstore,
4000 Fifth Ave.,
Oakland.

Right: Laurie London, 11, models wool throw-over. Left: Eight-day week calendar.

Tues Nov 18, 1982

Shopping With Polly

Survival Kits

Little metal boxes, put together just for fun, are of some use, too. Each holds a packet of chicken bouillon powder, a mild headache pill, a quick-wash towelette.

Then they specialize, with a tape measure for dieters, a tee for golfers, a tire patch for cyclists.

The tiny survival kits each cost $1.50.

Kards Unlimited
5522 Walnut St., Shadyside

Tues March 27, 1979

Shopping With Polly

Names that expand

Now you can buy balloons with the name of the birthday boy or girl or the guest of honor preprinted on them. They come in many colors, six to the $1.50 package.

Kards Unlimited,
5522 Walnut St.,
Shadyside.

Tues June 29, 1982

Clara Herron 1925-2007
Source: Post Gazette obituaries February 10, 2007

Polly, Clara, the unsung hero of early Kards Unlimited love and fanfare concretized in the archives of the Post-Gazette. How many people read her column, I wonder, to find some new lovely thing reviewed and worth the trip down to Kards for. The last two Polly columns I found were written by a different Polly and as far as I can tell - Polly stopped writing entirely in 2004.

Sue Giltenbooth

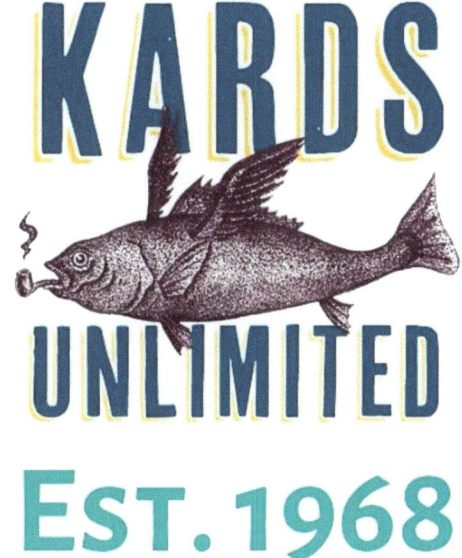

As mentioned, Kards Unlimited first opened in 1957 at 5513 Walnut St. Its modern legacy, however, began in 1968 when the business was purchased from Hallmark by Sue Giltenbooth, wcho would go on to operate Kards Unlimited until 1972.

At which point ownership was transferred to her daughter Mary Sue (left) son-in-law Ralph Colaizzi (below).

Mary Sue Colaizzi   Mary Sue and Ralph Colaizzi

Pittsburgh Post-Gazette

Magazine

TUESDAY, SEPTEMBER 25, 1990

ET CETERA

New shop in town

On Oct. 1, Counterpoint, in Loot's former space at One Oxford Centre, creation of Mary Sue and Ralph Colaizzi, will offer contemporary and traditional accessories as personal and corporate gifts. Each piece will have been chosen for quality, design, beauty and function. Designers include Aldo Rossi, Robert Venturi, Achille Castiglioni, Richard Sapper, Ettore Sottsass and Philippe Stark. The Colaizzis are already upbeat. They own Kards Unlimited and Ways and Means, Shadyside; Fan Mail, One Oxford Centre; Flying Colors and Paper Mill, Station Square; and Essex, Oakland. They also brought Department of the Interior to Pittsburgh, the upscale furniture store at the late lamented Motor Square Garden, East Liberty.

Pgh Post Gazette Tues Sept 25, 1990

Soon thereafter the Colaizzis would purchase the building at 5522 Walnut St and in 1974 move Kards Unlimited into its modern location. Quickly the Colaizzi's became known and respected for their business acumen and soon came to be the owners of multiple businesses in and around Pittsburgh; Ways and Means, The Paper Mill, Counterpoint & Kards Unlimited for example.

Scan QR code to be taken on a walking tour of Walnut St. in 1982!

W View Walnut St. "Ways And Means" on right   1982

Photographer: Art Steinmark

70

Then in 1994 ownership was transferred to Kristen Kershner, Mary Sue and Ralph Colaizzi's daughter. The irreplaceable and indescribably rad woman who owned and operated Kards Unlimited from 1994 until 2021 with her equally as rad husband Scott.

Pgh Magazine May 1998   Kristen and Scott Kershner

Few individuals, let alone couples, are as generous, empathetic, genuine and caring as these two. The legacy this family has created is one of light reflecting through decades of Pittsburgh hearts emanating joy in return. I'm grateful to know them.

Ralph Colaizzi with current owner Amanda Blair

Then in 2021 after 15 years of being an employee, ownership was transferred to my wife, Amanda Blair. Someone whose heart remains dedicated to the unique treasure that Pittsburgh has, since 1957, known Kards Unlimited to be.

She is also someone who purchased this business during a global respiratory pandemic...

But while proverbs say crisis is both equal parts danger and opportunity, Amanda Blair saw this time mainly as the latter. Throughout the early stages of the pandemic and with the help of web developer Melissa Morrill and her Kards Unlimited staff, Amanda set out to create a website that would aid in relieving the difficult doldrum of the daily quarantine faced by so many Pittsburghers.

For months Kards Unlimited staff delivered books, puzzles and games to anyone who needed them but couldn't leave their home.*

---

* In the very early stages of the pandemic I would drive puzzles and books to people's homes and make a little clowning show for the kids in the windows. I would get out of my car and put on bright yellow dishwashing gloves and a mask and make a big goofy deal out of using purell and some sanitizer spray on the packages. I got a few joyful chuckles through a few lonely windows so it was worth it.

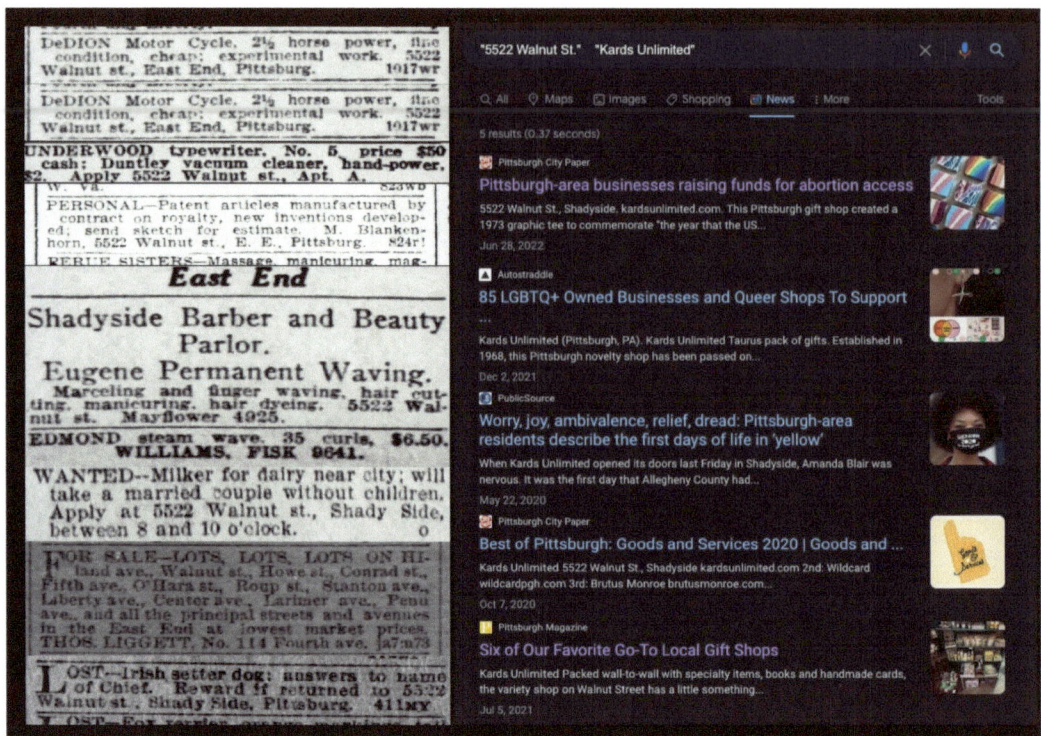

It is a strange place for me to be, here, at the end of this book trying to keep it simple. When I look at the contrast between 1890s newspaper clippings and 2022 Google searches I keep finding myself rambling down a long written road about my feelings towards my wife. How could I not?

How can I, her husband, not have something more in depth to say?

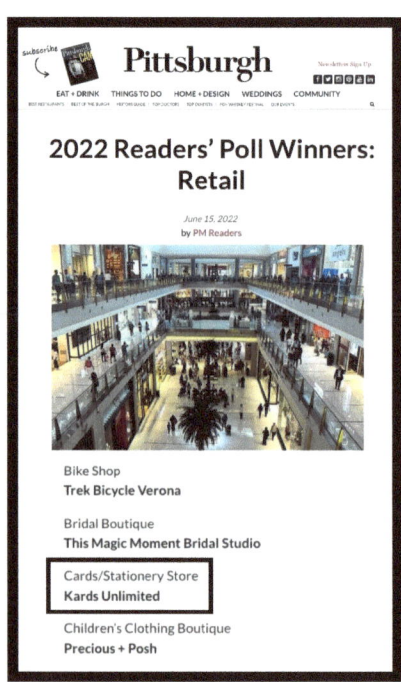

I did. I said it. It's this book. If you are, or anyone is, here reading this line you have made it through a quest of love. I wrote this book to be closer to my wife.

It worked.

At the end of this book, the current state of 5522 Walnut St. here in July of 2022, Kards Unlimited is being awarded Best Local Card Shop in the Pittsburgh Magazine 2022 Reader's Poll.

How fitting.

Amanda Blair
2022
Photo: City Paper Photographer Jared Wickerham

Amanda Blair.

Owner of Kards Unlimited at 5522 Walnut St.

Afterword

Now what?

Now we grow and change again. We face crises as opportunity and opportunity as growth. We slough off the sepia tone of the past. Repair the broken parts of our photographs and upscale the stories told within them. We make sure to always keep coffee and family close by. I wonder what kind of future waits for Kards Unlimited and Walnut St. to discover it.

I look through all of my photos collected along this journey and can see the change happening throughout time. Where the Lemon Tree Shop and Clay Place stood at Ivy and Walnut is now a large, brick, development. The same as where The Music Emporium, Call Me Mister and Yogurt Works sat on Bellefonte and Walnut. Both gas stations are gone. The movie theater is now a lulu lemon.

I think of asking all of the same questions that Barbara Cloud asked but I know the search for any kind of answer is silly. The wheel turns. We are seasonal creatures. Change occurs out of our control and nothing can remain the same for very long.

I think I like it that way.

I think I want to leave it on a simple note.

Love spans the change of eons, let this book be a pause in space time.

Jason M. Kirin

Digital and Physical Museum

This project was meant to be simple, uncover a non-modern photograph of 5522 Walnut St., restore it, frame it, present it as a birthday gift and move on. Well, here we are. A simple restoration turned into months of work digging through the archives of Historic Pittsburgh, the Carnegie Museum, the University of Pittsburgh Library, Chatham University Archives, the Heinz History Center, the Shadyside Chamber of Commerce, Ancestry.com, Reddit, Carnegie Mellon University Library and few special collections provided to me by individuals I either met through Facebook or had already known.

Each of these archives revealed unique treasures causing profound connections and impressions.

However, it was the Facebook group known as Friends from Shadyside that provided (and continues to provide) the most help in the creation of this book, the videos and photo restorations.

A few members in particular I need to mention...

Mark B. Morrow, who in order to help identify the chronology of these photos, would comment on the year, make and model of, literally, every car in every picture.

Paul Corbett, a member who brought a camera along with him to an Arts Festival and the Pirates win of the World Series in 1979 both being celebrated on Walnut St.

James William, the original Walnut St. historian. His photos, postcards, menus and memorabilia still hang in the basement of Cappy's for everyone to see.

Judy Conri Saldi sent me the most stunning photo of her aunt and uncle on their wedding day in 1955 standing on the sidewalk on Walnut St. In the comment section of this photo her and her cousin recollect, together, their love for their aunt.

Photo source: Judy Conroy Saldi   2022 Photo Restoration: Jason Kirin

Marc V. Rock-Steady, an already good friend of mine. Marc sent me a message saying he'd found a box of slides marked "1970s Walnut St." Marc is a member of the Indovina family line. The Indovinas had a fruit market on Walnut St. in the 1940s. These slides were all pristine and beautifully reflected a few 1970s days on Walnut St.

I have never developed or scanned slides before. I had no idea what to do with them.

I tried a flat bed scanner. I took a photo of them over a light box. None of these were satisfactory.

None of these created the quality I required.

I found a gadget from Magnasonic that would scan any kind of slide and any kind of negative, turning them into digitized photos within seconds.

The quality imagery it produces overwhelms any expectation I could have had.

The scanner allows me to scan each slide at multiple exposure levels which is really convenient because when I layer the multiple exposure levels together in Pixelmator I get to toggle the light and color in every which way I want.

Then I give them new skies in an app called Motionleap.

Amira Badran Lopes, a dear friend whose grandmother grew up on Ivy St and was fond of taking pictures of the early 1900s 5th Ave. mansions. Amira allowed me to scan all of the photos from this fragile album. Some of these photos are Shadyside Churchs and also of of 5th Ave. mansions that are no longer there.

3rd Presbyterian Church

Church of the Ascension

Hostetler Residence 5th Avenue

Home of Dr J W Anderson

Art Steinmark mailed me an envelope of 20 black and white negatives. The photographs were a series he took of two of his friends in 1982 walking up Filbert St. coming out onto Walnut St. and chatting in front of Kards Unlimited for a while. Art and I sent messages back and forth for a few weeks deciding on how these photos should be presented. We came up with the 1982 walking tour of Walnut St. featured in the Kards Unlimited section of this book.

Tom Doyle is an absolute trip and one of the coolest people I've met along this journey. Through the Friends from Shadyside Facebook group Tom sent me a message letting me know I'd want his photos. Back in the 1970s he lived at 5509 Walnut St. 2nd floor. Tom was a photographer and his whole thing was "people of Walnut St." With Kards Unlimited behind a perpetual blind spot he'd hang out his window all day taking pictures of people. Yelling down and inviting them up for a joint and a laugh. Tom's pictures are truly amazing and while a few of them are in this book, the rest of them are in the Facebook group. We still often text each other and occasionally he'll stop in at Kards Unlimited to show me some new negatives he uncovered. Or to tell me some story he remembered.

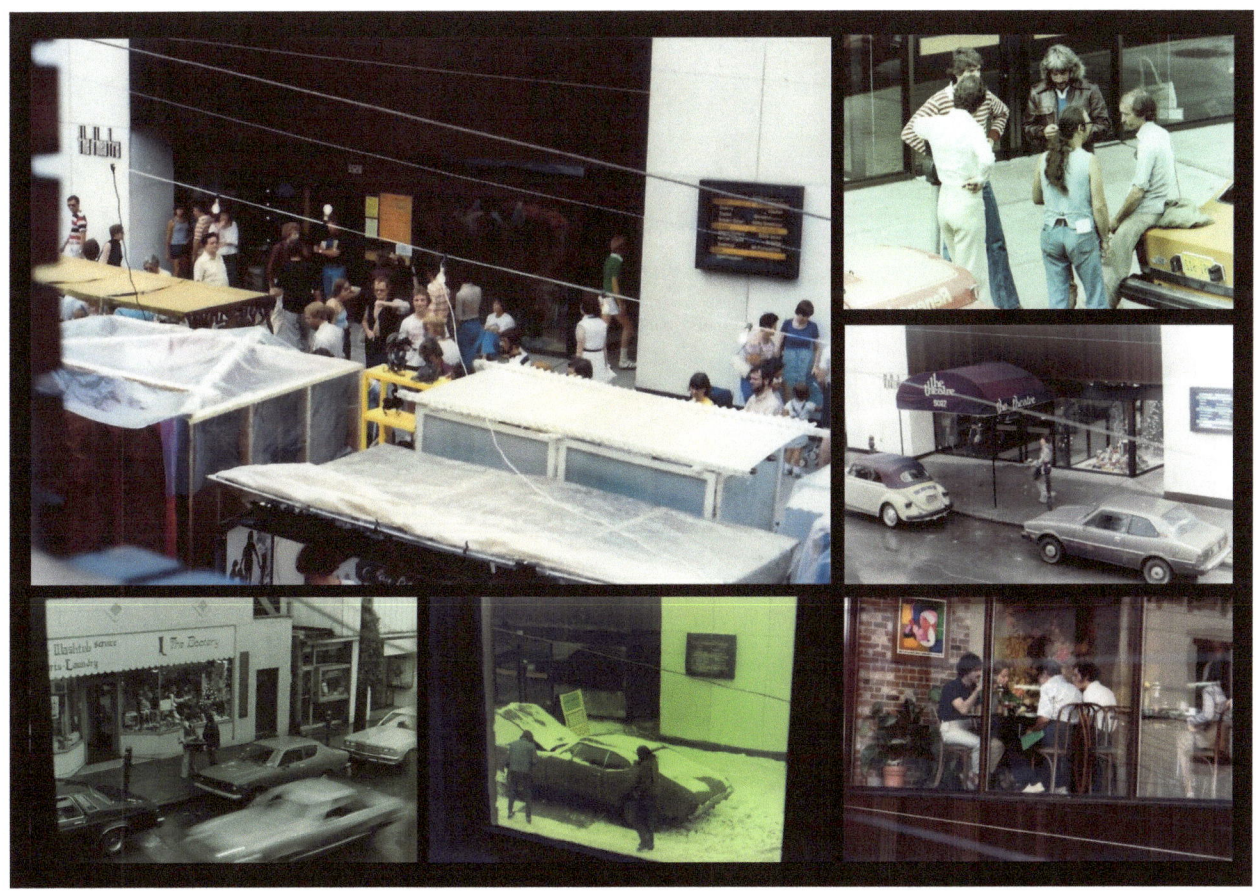

From across the archives mentioned I was able to uncover roughly 100 non-modern photographs of Walnut St. spanning from 1935-1985. Throughout the months of 2022 I spent much of my spare time focused on restoring these photos.

Here is why I have decided not to include most of them in this book...

When each photograph was restored to a quality I felt comfortable with, I would post it to the Friends from Shadyside Facebook group and just watch. I'd read, comment and enter into dialogue with people who actually lived within those moments. People who actually lived within these photographs!

Every time I posted a photo the comment section would explode before me. Scores of stories would pour in; people reminiscing about what it was like to work in these places, what the people were like who loved and lived there. The commonality is how much they cared about being there.

As long as Facebook remains, so too will these stories, these truly real moments explained by the truly genuine humans that lived them. They don't belong in this book. They belong there.

A few restored images of buildings I posted were buildings that I couldn't recognize but soon learned were cherished locations demolished by developers in the 90s. People hadn't seen these buildings since then. People hadn't felt these feelings, been flooded with these memories since then.

In that frame of heart, and mind, people commented on these photos. Those comments moved me... Often to elation. Most often to gratitude. I could find myself there. In these photos with these people! The supplemental material provided by this community through the comment sections of these photos is, I feel, essential for the full experience and exploration of them. So in that community is where the digital museum of Walnut St. shall remain.

The physical museum however... The art and photos regarding 5522 Walnut St., can only be found by exploring the shelves of Kards Unlimited. You'll find the Fay Moore painting there, Art Steinmark's photos there and also a few other goodies I won't spoil.

Here are instructions on accessing the Friends from Shadyside / digital museum.

Here is the link

https://www.facebook.com/groups/581787848508196/

or

Login to Facebook.com and search for the group "Friends from Shadyside"
In the "media" section of the group you will find the entirety of images I have
uncovered from the archives above.

or

Scan this QR Code ⟶

So that is where these photos will be viewable, in the community that produced so many
of the originals - coupled with the stories and memories connected to them.

Visit the stories, take them in, read and engage in the comments. They are a wonderful
community there. If Facebook is inaccessible to you, email me and I'll link you to the
Google drive album.

Lastly, the digital museum is an organism. It will grow continuously. Please feel free to
reach out to me at ShadysideHistory@Gmail.com if you have any photos or material
regarding Shadyside you would like to have restored, colorized, etc. and added into the
archives.

Jason M. Kirin

Archivist Acknowledgment.

Carnegie Museum.
The Carnegie Museum archivist Gil Pietrzak uncovered the photo of the Kards Unlimited storefront at 5513 Walnut St. after it had been buried in a folder since it had been developed.

The Heinz History Center
Kelly George, a Project Archivist at the Heinz History Center Detre Library was absolutely instrumental in some of the finer details of this project. Through multiple back and forth emails she led me to all of the tools necessary to access, search and understand census data. She led me to Polk's City Directories and spent an afternoon searching through a few decades worth looking for any listings available for the Village Treat Shop and Benzenhoefer's Barbershop. She also helped me understand the huge map collection available at the Detre Library.

Chatham University Archives
Molly Tighe. Archivist who fully understood my project as soon as I reached out to her regarding George Gibson. While we still have yet to uncover a further connection between Gibson and Chatham/PCW Molly continues to dig and continues to send me photos she uncovers from the archives. Photos that connect Chatham to the greater Shadyside area.

Lisa Benzenhoefer
The Great-Great-Grandaughter of Gottlieb and Caroline who is as invested in the research as I am. We constantly share and chat about Benzenhoefer research. As of this writing Lisa and other Benzenhoefers are trying to track down a photo from Freda's wedding, which was listed as having happened at 5522.

Indispensable Websites.
ArcGIS.com
HistoricPittsburgh.org
Retrographer.org
Newspapers.com
Ancestry.com
MyHeritage.com

5522 Walnut St. Residential and Commercial Timeline

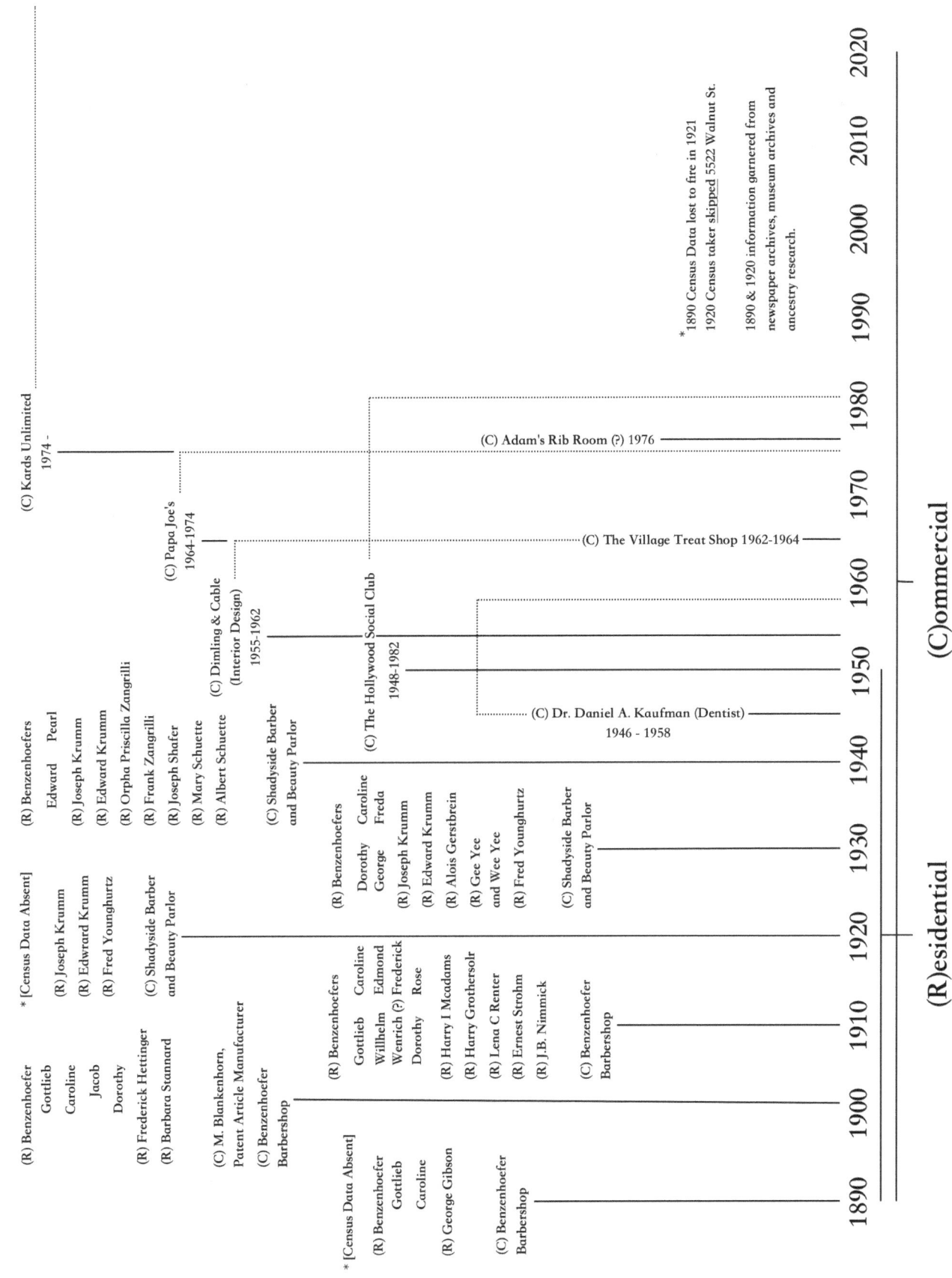

(R) Benzenhoefer
Gottlieb
Caroline
Jacob
Dorothy

(R) Frederick Hettinger

(R) Barbara Stannard

(C) M. Blankenhorn,
Patent Article Manufacturer

(C) Benzenhoefer
Barbershop

*[Census Data Absent]

(R) Benzenhoefer
Gottlieb
Caroline

(R) George Gibson

(C) Benzenhoefer
Barbershop

(R) Benzenhoefers
Gottlieb   Caroline
Willhelm   Edmond
Wenrich (?) Frederick
Dorothy   Rose

(R) Harry I Mcadams

(R) Harry Grothersolr

(R) Lena C Renter

(R) Ernest Strohm

(R) J.B. Nimmick

(C) Benzenhoefer
Barbershop

* [Census Data Absent]

(R) Joseph Krumm

(R) Edward Krumm

(R) Fred Younghurtz

(C) Shadyside Barber
and Beauty Parlor

(R) Benzenhoefers
Dorothy   Caroline
George   Freda

(R) Joseph Krumm

(R) Edward Krumm

(R) Alois Gerstbrein

(R) Gee Yee
and Wee Yee

(R) Fred Younghurtz

(C) Shadyside Barber
and Beauty Parlor

(R) Benzenhoefers
Edward   Pearl

(R) Joseph Krumm

(R) Edward Krumm

(R) Orpha Priscilla Zangrilli

(R) Frank Zangrilli

(R) Joseph Shafer

(R) Mary Schuette

(R) Albert Schuette

(C) Shadyside Barber
and Beauty Parlor

(C) Kards Unlimited
1974 -

(C) Papa Joe's
1964-1974

(C) Dimling & Cable
(Interior Design)
1955-1962

(C) The Hollywood Social Club
1948-1982

(C) Adam's Rib Room (?) 1976

(C) The Village Treat Shop 1962-1964

(C) Dr. Daniel A. Kaufman (Dentist)
1946 - 1958

1890   1900   1910   1920   1930   1940   1950   1960   1970   1980   1990   2000   2010   2020

(R)esidential   (C)ommercial

*1890 Census Data lost to fire in 1921
1920 Census taker skipped 5522 Walnut St.

1890 & 1920 information garnered from
newspaper archives, museum archives and
ancestry research.